THE PRESCHOOL PARENT PRIMER

PRACTICAL ADVICE & RESOURCES FOR PARENTS, CAREGIVERS, & TEACHERS OF PRESCHOOLERS

PAMELA EVANS

IVYARTZ

Copyright © 2021 IvyArtz
The Preschool Parent Primer Third Edition
By Pamela Evans www.IvyArtz.com

All rights reserved. No part of this book may be used or reproduced without written permission from IvyArtz Publications, P.O. Box 620, Ivy, VA 22945
Names and situations in the book have been changed and are composites of situations and people to protect the privacy of each individual.

The Preschool Parent Primer is a resource guide and is not a substitute for consultation with appropriate professionals (family doctor, therapist, or local social services) when dealing with serious issues.

Other IvyArtz publications:
The Preschool Parent Blog and *The Preschool Parent Book Review*

ISBN: 978-0-9980969-3-3

CONTENTS

Dedication	v
Preface	vii
Introduction	ix
1. Discovering Preschool	1
2. Routines	17
3. What to Look For in a Preschool	31
4. Specific Curricula	54
5. What is Developmentally Appropriate?	64
6. The Parent-Teacher Partnership	83
7. Worries and Fears	100
8. Toilet Training & Tantrums	121
9. The Arts and Exploration	135
10. Kindergarten	147
Epilogue	154
Bibliography	157
Recommended Children's Stories	161
Acknowledgments	163
About the Author	165

To the families of C-Street Preschool,
and to my family.
Thank you.

Preschoolers working at take-apart table.

PREFACE

Welcome to *The Preschool Parent Primer*. It's here to provide you with practical advice from my many years of teaching preschoolers, developing curricula, and working with parents.

A book cannot tell you how to raise your child or what's right for your family. Every family is unique. You are the expert on your child, but perspective from someone who's seen many children and families through these early years can be helpful. The best advice is to trust your intuition, seek council from those you trust, and don't worry about the minor stuff. Take the time to enjoy these years. Cliché or not, the preschool years will be over before you know it, and you will hardly remember many of the issues that seem insurmountable now. That said, here is some help for now.

This book is a guide toward best practices for parents and teachers of preschoolers. The purpose of *The Preschool Parent Primer* is to provide some insight into many common practices of teachers, concerns of parents, and needs of preschoolers. Chapters begin with a list of key factors to keep in mind and ideas to help with a specific challenge.

The chapter following the list has in-depth information on the topic with anecdotes and references for additional reading.

Parents are a child's first and most influential teachers; however, parenting and teaching can be challenging, as each has a steep learning curve. This book is my checklist of information for starting each school year as a preschool teacher, along with useful advice for parents.

The Preschool Parent Primer is a resource guide. You will find links to books, websites, and products throughout the book. I am not affiliated with any of the companies. The links are just here to make your life easier!

INTRODUCTION

Generally, an introduction lays out what you will be reading in the book. Many books on preschoolers are based on specific studies or specific developmental philosophies. I feel an obligation to let you know right away that, aside from sources to those materials in the bibliography, this book is intentionally designed differently. Although it is a list of best practices, *The Preschool Parent Primer* is more of a conversation about many issues that concern parents including: what to look for in a preschool; how to develop a positive parent-teacher relationship; what normal behavior for a particular age looks like; and the importance of routines, socialization, regular sleep, and more.

Each chapter starts with a list of key factors. This handy summary of the chapter is placed at the beginning of the chapter for easy reference when challenges pop up.

I hope *The Preschool Parent Primer* will give you some peace of mind about what to expect during these years and that it will provide some ideas and resources for ways to address the challenges that will arise as your child steps out into a larger world.

Backyard obstacle course fun!

A brief note on pronouns; (she, he, they) I wish the English language had a commonly used gender-neutral pronoun. It currently does not, although *they* is becoming more frequent in use. For readability, I chose to alternate pronouns by chapter.

1
DISCOVERING PRESCHOOL

Key Factors:

Realize how well you are already parenting.

Allow your child to take on new and more challenging real jobs.

The goal is happy, healthy, independent children.

We often associate happiness in life with how well one can understand and negotiate social situations.

Preschool can be a wonderful way to build a community for your entire family, not just your child.

Scheduling play dates with other children is one of the best things you can do for your child.

Socially, children learn more from a peer than from an adult.

The most important job in preschool, for children, teachers, and parents, is socialization.

Playing with others is a process requiring many steps that adults often take for granted.

It is important to listen to your child and show respect for her thoughts and feelings.

Upsetting social interactions are pathways to learning and empathy.

Play! Play! Play!

Within the pages of *The Preschool Parent Primer,* you will find some advice, some examples, and a lot of encouragement. My hope is you will **realize how well you are already parenting.** The practical advice and useful tips within these pages should reinforce your belief that you are doing a good job. Parenting is difficult. You already have wisdom to be a great parent for your child because no one knows your child like you do. Take a little time each day to think about what worked best for your child and what didn't work so well. Each day is a work in progress. A little reflection can provide a great deal of insight.

You have a preschooler in your home. You don't have time to read the great American novel! *The Preschool Parent Primer* is set up with that reality in mind. It's designed to help put your mind at ease. The chapters are brief with tips on best practices and resource lists where appropriate. A list of *Key Factors* starts each chapter and helps you find or revisit topics of interest.

This book focuses on the preschool years, when your child is ready to move out into a bigger world beyond home and daycare. When referring to preschool age in this book, the focus is on children who are ready for preschool activities. It's about maturity, not chronological age, but generally children need to be 2 years 6 months or 3 years of age for traditional preschool.

It's an exciting time when children are rapidly expanding their knowledge, shaping opinions about their world, and figuring out their place in it.

Children can help at home with proper tasks. It may take you twice as long to get something done with your child's help. Your patience now will strengthen your child's capabilities and confidence in the future. Basic hands-on chores help a child feel like a useful, contributing member of the family. During these early years, reassess how much your child can do regularly. **Allow your child to take on new and more challenging real jobs.**

Tools their size can help. For Example, a small broom allows your child to have success in sweeping the floor. I was the youngest of several children; my mother had jobs for each child, depending on age and ability. One of my first jobs was to dust. Dusting may sound easy, but my mother expected the job to be done well. Treat chores as an important contribution to the family.

One thing you don't want to do is push inappropriate academic skills too early. Many studies have shown that young children need to learn and practice life skills. They need time to explore their environment. Pushing early academic skills can backfire in the long run. We will go in depth on this matter in Chapter 5, *What Is "Developmentally Appropriate?"*

While reading a well-known parenting magazine, I came across an article on what your child should know before going to preschool. The author went over many skills children learn in preschool. These are not prerequisites. A good preschool will meet children where they are socially, cognitively, and physically.

Modern society is always thinking ahead instead of focusing on the present. It often forces lessons on our children earlier than is appropriate. This type of parenting and schooling can lead to the opposite of what parents want for their children.

For most of us, **the goal is happy, healthy, independent children.** The independent part is the key, and it is often the onerous part for parents. It's difficult to give up control and allow children to grow at their own rate. My hope is *The Preschool Parent Primer* will provide you with tools and resources to make the preschool years a little easier, more relaxed, and fun. So let's begin.

Is preschool necessary? Not always. Many children don't attend formal preschool. Some parents do an outstanding job of including their child in everyday tasks and playgroups before heading off to Kindergarten. The key is involvement with other children. Playing well with others is an important life skill. Preschool is where children learn to negotiate social situations. **We often associate happiness in life with how well one can understand and negotiate social situations.**

When your child goes to preschool, she may discover some of her own likes and dislikes. Your child's choices may surprise you. For example, dynamic, active play may intrigue a very quiet child, giving the mistaken impression that she may fear the play. She may be trying to figure out how to join in. A child who is loud and active at home can be so excited to be at school that she is quiet while taking in the new atmosphere. Try not to make assumptions about your child's feelings as her world expands.

Patience is key during acclimation to a new school or play situation. It is important to ask your child what she thinks and try to listen to her exact words without reading your predispositions into her new world. If she is nervous about the new play routine, you need to be a calm, supportive guide. Explain to your child that everyone is nervous in new situations. Let her know who to talk to if she has a problem or question and you are not there.

A few years ago, a parent of one of my students told me that she, the parent, was bullied in school during her childhood. The mother came to me, concerned her child might be the victim of another child at the school. She relayed that her daughter, Maddy, said that Liam was really crazy. I hadn't noticed any problem between the two children on the playground, but I did often see Maddy watching Liam. I talked to Maddy about Liam. It turned out that Maddy wanted to play with him. She was not used to super energetic, exciting play, like Liam's fast running games. Maggie didn't have the skills to join the game. It just took a little coaching on how to ask Liam if she could join in. They became fast friends at school, followed by many play dates. Maddy's mom was relieved.

Preschool is a time to move into a larger community. A child's world goes beyond family and friends to an expanded group at school. It can be stressful for the child and the parents. Now your child has outside influences. Other families may eat foods your child has never seen, they may talk differently, or handle conflicts in a different way.

It can be a challenging time for parents at first, but it's the opportune time to let your child know why your family does things the way you do. You may get new ideas for your family, so try to keep an open mind. **Preschool can be a wonderful way to build a community for your entire family, not just your child.**

Preschool can bring some anxiety for both parent and child. The more anxious you are, the more anxious your child will be. You need to find a school you feel comfortable with, so your child will feel comfortable too.

In chapter 3, we focus on what to look for in a preschool. For now, let's focus on why to send a child to a preschool. No one has to go to preschool, but in today's busy world if you find the right school for your child it can mean finding community and support for the whole family. For some preschool is a choice, for others a necessity. The goal is to find the best fit for your situation.

Keep in mind that you are the expert on your child. A preschool should provide you with professional teachers who can help support you with their knowledge of childhood development. Qualified, caring adults working with your child can be an immeasurable aid when you are having parenting challenges that cause both you and your child to become distressed.

A calm, outside influence can help guide and encourage you and your child. This is the big difference between play dates and playgroups (which are also wonderful) and attending a preschool run by competent professionals.

Scheduling play dates with other children is one of the best things you can do for your child. Play is how children learn all about their world. Play is much more important to your child than a new toy or computer game. During the preschool years, play is how we learn everything from language and counting to skipping and pumping on a swing. Play with other children is how children build social skills.

Play has changed over the years. I'm not advocating that it was better in the past or that it is better now, but times have changed. Preschool teachers will tell you that even in the past decade there has been a dramatic change in the social abilities of children coming into school. Large families, which provided more sibling interaction, are less common, as is free play in the neighborhood.

Children are less likely to have a lot of playtime with children of different ages and backgrounds. And children almost never have unsupervised play, which used to be quite normal.

In some respects, this can be beneficial. More supervision means safer and kinder play. On the other hand, it's surprising how many children are at a loss when they want to approach a new friend. Many children don't know what to say or do when they want to join other children. They are used to adults handling the introductions for them.

Playing with other children takes practice. A child needs to make social mistakes to understand how to get in there and play. Adults are often more sensitive and upset, than their child, when watching their child try to join a group of children and being told "No." If as a parent, you always intercede to make sure everyone is nice, your child will not learn to make social decisions for herself. She may not feel competent in playgroups and her feelings will be easily hurt.

It is important to model kind behavior and words, but you want your child to figure out how to stand up for herself and make independent decisions. These social skills require practice. Talk briefly to your child after a negative social encounter. Together you can practice what to say or do if a similar situation occurs in the future.

Many children are socialized with adults who let them have the toy or win the game. **Socially, children learn more from a peer than from an adult.** How do you deal with someone who is difficult or mean? How can you stand up for yourself? How can you share the same toy? How does it feel to be left out? How do you like being the leader? Why can't you hit someone? These are all lessons learned through play.

A parent told me about a playground incident she experienced. It sums up some current issues regarding independence for young children. The mother, Jean, was sitting talking with some friends while her 3-year-old daughter, Ella, played and then fell off a climber on the playground. The mother watched and continued to talk with the other parents.

Jean had to stop another parent from running over to Ella. The 3-year-old sat for a minute, then stood up, and brushed off her leg. She got right back up on the climber. It's not about being harsh or not caring for a hurt child. It is about parents allowing children to grow and handle situations on their own. Jean could see her child was not hurt. As a parent, Jean wants Ella to learn to take care of herself. She also knows Ella will ask for help when she needs it.

The most important job in preschool, for children, teachers, and parents, is socialization. This is where we learn how to get along well with others. In preschool, we learn we can disagree and still be friends.

Let's move on to how preschool teachers handle play. There will be more information in Chapter 5, *The Role of the Preschool Teacher*.

Teachers want to help all the children learn how to negotiate play together. Some children have a hard time joining into play with their peers so we help them find and practice phrases like, "Can I be the cat?" or even just "Can I play with you?" Sometimes we help them join the game by bringing food to the pretend firehouse (especially if they want to play, but going out on a fire run is a little too exciting). We help children to join in at music time or at clean up time. It can be slow going at first. A child might need to watch the activity for a while. It takes repetition and practice to learn to work in a group.

Sharing can be quite a tricky undertaking for many preschoolers. Like any skill, it requires practice. A child who grabs a toy out of another child's hand needs to practice asking for a turn. When asking for a turn, the child may need support and guidance. This is especially true if the other child doesn't agree to their request. **Playing with others is a process requiring many steps that adults often take for granted.** Children who always get their way do not learn to negotiate and play with other children in a fulfilling way.

So how do adults help? For starters, it's important not to talk too much. Children become deaf to an adult repeating the same thing over and over. Modeling appropriate words and behavior is much more effective and respectful of the child.

Parents often wonder if their child understands what is being asked of her. This concern can cause adults to over explain and confuse their child. If a child may not hit anyone, then an extensive discussion is not needed. Do I want to understand what frustration drove a child to hit another child or adult? Yes, I do, but it's not a long conversation. The situation needs to be acknowledged and remedied.

Your calm, clear behavior is more effective and understandable for children. A long conversation often means you are open to debate on the issue. Stay calm; choose your words wisely. You don't need to restate something if it is not open for debate.

Your child already knows what to do. She's just trying to figure out if it is possible to change your mind. If your child is emotional and upset, continuing to talk to her will not help because she is feeling, not thinking. Give her some time and space to regroup before asking questions or giving explanations.

It is important to listen to your child and show respect for her thoughts and feelings. It's all about balance. Discuss situations with your child and listen to your child's perspective. When health, safety, or important, established rules are concerned, too much talking can confuse the issue for your child.

Really listening to your child is key. Try not to read things into your child's words. It's easy to misunderstand a child's concern and read your own experience or feelings into what your child is saying.

One morning, Jenny was crying while looking at Diego. Diego stood there, staring at Jenny, not saying a word. It looked like Diego (a much bigger child) had done something to Jenny. The teacher asked both children what happened. This required giving Jenny some time to calm down.

It turned out that Diego was playing with a stuffed dog, and Jenny wanted the dog. Jenny, only 3 years old, reacted physically, a common trait in preschoolers. Instead of using her words and asking Diego if she could play with the dog, she bit him on the arm and grabbed the dog. As soon as she bit Diego, she knew she shouldn't have. She threw the dog at Diego and burst into tears. Diego just stood there, confused and hurt.

The teacher tended to Diego and he expressed his feelings. He described what happened from his perspective. Diego said he was fine. He also said Jenny could have the dog if she wanted. The teacher asked Diego to hang onto the dog for now and play.

Then the teacher talked to Jenny. It was clear from Jenny's response that she was as shocked as Diego. She couldn't believe she had bitten him! Jenny told Diego she was sorry and would not bite him again. Together, the teacher and Jenny practiced the words she needed to ask for a turn. The teacher also asked Jenny, "What can you do if Diego doesn't want to give you a turn right away?" Jenny decided she could play with the duck puzzle.

To my knowledge, Jenny never bit again (not always the case in these situations), but she did struggle with frustration for some time. If she did not get what she wanted right away, her little body would tense up. It was inspiring to watch her learn to calm herself, take a breath, and negotiate with others to get a turn. This is an example of the type of life skills children practice in preschool.

It takes time and patience to master social skills. You only get to work on these skills when things go wrong. As hard as it is for adults to hear, **upsetting social interactions are pathways to learning and empathy.** Adults want children to have a fun, happy day at school, but if nothing goes wrong socially, nothing is learned.

Your child is a preschooler and may not understand what is happening, like Diego. If something upsetting has happened, try to listen to your child, and any children involved. Hear what is actually being said. Don't read more into their words, even if you think you saw everything that happened. Adults tend to read situations differently than children.

Here's an interesting fact. It is not uncommon for adults to hang onto negative emotions longer than preschoolers. Your child may have a complete breakdown because Timmy hit her. Five minutes later she runs up to Timmy and asks him to help build a plane with the big blocks. They are off having a great time together, and you're still upset.

Try to stay in the moment. Are you going to keep an eye out for trouble? Yes, but try not to hold a grudge against a 3-year-old who is learning how to play. Tomorrow your child may be the one who behaves inappropriately, and will need the guidance of patient adults.

Sometimes parents have concerns regarding praise and children. Rather than promoting any one theory, I believe moderation is key. You can find entire books on just this topic. Many contradict each other. Moderation and knowing your child are the important factors.

One language theory states that children and their creative projects should not be praised at all. The idea being the child should find the value of her work intrinsically and not seek outside praise. This is a tempting and valuable philosophy, when noticing the myriad of events in which children are given false praise. When trophies are handed out, just for showing up, trophies become worthless.

We want children to develop their own sense of worth and not rely on others for their confidence. Be careful with praise. Compliments should be used sparingly and they should be genuine. Again, every family must find their own balance depending on their beliefs and their child's nature. Try not to go to extremes.

Tyrus was one of only two preschool children who asked me regularly if his paintings were *good*. *Good* is a vague term we rarely employ to describe our work in preschool. Tyrus was from a family that had concerns about giving praise. Were they concerned because he wanted praise so much, or did he need the praise at school because he didn't receive it any at home?

Just keep in mind every child is different and everyone needs to feel valued. Instead of telling your child her painting is good, try some open-ended questions and listen to her answers. That shows her you are interested in what she is doing.

Listen to your child and encourage her to think about her projects with questions. "What is happening in your painting?" "What do you like about your art project?" "Let's both paint with those colors." Nothing encourages your child more than seeing you follow her lead.

Play! Play! Play! So many children need more play. Play with other children. Our lives are so busy and it's harder to send young children out to play in the neighborhood. It's not always easy to arrange, but children need to play with other children on a regular basis. The more varied your child's play experiences are, the more she will learn.

Play with older children differs from playing with younger children. Both are beneficial and help with all kinds of social constructs. Different age play helps with learning how to join the group, how to lead, how to compromise, and how to hold your ground.

One family told me they would only attend events if they were sure that at least one child in attendance was the same age as their child. Why limit your child's social experience in that way. Give your child the opportunity to grow and try on different social roles.

How do you build confidence? How do you learn to negotiate? How do you learn to comfort yourself when someone is mean? How to you learn to stand up for yourself? How do you learn to empathize? If you're a preschooler, the answer is simple; play with other children. Play with new friends, old friends, older children, younger children. Play! Play! Play!

Stream play at *Wildrock*. An outdoor playscape in Crozet, VA. Photo credit: Kat Werner.

You are the expert on your child even if some days you don't feel like it. After seeing so many students grow into confident, happy, young adults, I have noted the things those families have in common and included their advice within the following pages.

Adults can help young children find their voices, strengths, and independence. We can also help children learn how to handle the challenges they face. In most cases, helping a child to grow requires adults knowing when to step back.

Children need to be allowed freedom to fall, fail, and experiment on their own. As parents and teachers in the lives of young children, we can guide them, but children must be allowed room to grow and discover things for themselves. Adults who worry and hover over children create dependent young adults. Our children are like mirrors. Your stress is their stress. Your confidence is their confidence.

Further Reading for Parents

Lythcott-Haims, Julie. *How to Raise an Adult: Break Free of the Overparenting Trap and Prepare Your Kid For Success*. (Henry Holt and Company, LLC, 2015).

Bronson, Po & Merryman, Ashley. *NurtureShock; New Thinking About Children*. (Hachette Book Group, 2009).

Brown, Stuart & Vaughan, Christopher. *Play: How It Shapes the Brain, Opens the Imagination, and Invigorates the Soul*. (Penguin Group, 2009).

To find the right size tools for helping around the house check out www.forsmallhands.com

Books to Share with Your Child

Robinson, Christian. *You Matter*. (Atheneum Books for Young Readers, 2020).

2

ROUTINES

IN SUPPORT OF HEALTHY MINDS, HEARTS AND BODIES.

Key Factors:

A daily routine allows for peace of mind.

A good morning routine works for the entire family.

Outdoor time should be a part of your child's daily routine.

Preschools have to meet the needs of many children simultaneously.

For young children, there can be a significant amount of stress in not knowing what will be expected of them during the day.

Is everyone getting plenty of sleep?

Learning to be comfy, secure, and able to get to sleep will be a skill that your child will use the rest of his life.

Reassessing routines is vital to avoid frustrating your child, and to continue developing independence and confidence.

Down time should be part of your routine.

One of the great life skills a parent can give a child is learning how to be flexible and adaptive.

It would be hard to overstate the importance of routines for preschoolers. For young children, each day is full of new ideas and experiences. There are few times in life when one's body and brain grow at such a rapid rate. Every day is full of change.

Routines are an important stabilizing influence. Children, like adults, get frustrated when they do not know what to expect or when their expectations are not met. **A daily routine allows for the peace of mind** that comes from knowing what is going to happen. A routine provides the opportunity for expectations to be met.

Routines give a child a sense of control. It doesn't mean we can't break the routine from time to time. That's just as important as having a routine. Some days don't go the way you want or expect them to go.

Learning patience and flexibility is another life lesson. We will address breaking routines at the end of this chapter.

Morning Routines

A good start in the morning makes for a better day. Your morning routine is not just for your preschooler. The routine should help everyone start the day, even if family members are tired or upset.

A good routine gives a child a calm, consistent way to begin the day and a way to know there will be time with a parent, time for choices, and food! Morning routines vary depending on your family and your child. Your routine should be flexible and change as your growing child can take on more responsibility.

An organized start to the day at home gives your child the best start to his preschool day as well.

A good morning routine works for the entire family. Here are a few things to think about as you establish one that works for your family. Everyone needs some time to get going in the morning. This means getting enough sleep and perhaps prepping some things the night before. What parts of your morning are difficult? Clothing choices? Breakfast choices?

What can you do the night before? Are there parts of the morning routine your child can be invested in? As children grow, they can help with more of the morning routine. They can also make more decisions on their own that fit into the requirements and time parameters you provide.

Many families have morning check lists allowing older children to understand and help meet the tasks required of them in the morning on their own. Their tasks may even include helping younger family members.

Preschoolers, however, need your clear guidance and just a few choices. If each morning is a huge negotiation, you don't have a comforting morning routine.

What can your child do independently? If he picks out clothes with you the night before, can he put them on in the morning himself? Maybe after he puts his pants on, he calls you to help with his shirt. It's all very individual depending on motor skills, where you are with potty training, and how independent your child is.

The bottom line is; encourage that independent streak and reassess often. If he can put on his clothes, but the shirt is on backwards, who cares? He'll figure that out eventually, but if you are always correcting everything your child does, he may well get frustrated and not want to even try.

It is faster for you to dress him, but that doesn't provide growth for either of you. Allow time for your child to do the things he can do while you take care of other things that need your attention in the morning.

Breakfast can be a tricky part of the morning routine. What options work best for your family? Some families prepare food the night before, so they can reheat or just grab and go in the morning. Can your child help you set the table for breakfast as part of your evening routine?

It's easy to make food assumptions at breakfast, thinking that only certain foods like eggs or cereal will do. For people in Japan, fish and rice are a common breakfast. In Thailand, spicy fish with sweet and spicy pork is common. Some Germans enjoy wursts, cheese, and bread for their morning meal. A nutritious breakfast with protein is important for your child. As long as everyone is eating some good food, who cares if it's *breakfast food?*

It's nice to have the time to sit down together and eat instead of spending the morning preparing the food and gobbling it down, or worse, skipping breakfast. Try not to be the parent that prepares things for everyone else and then doesn't eat. In the long run, that behavior is not good for you. It can make you cranky and it sets a poor example for your child.

Model the type of adult you want your child to become and give yourself a break at the same time.

I want to reinforce the concept that an effective morning routine helps to give you and your child a better chance for a calm, productive day at school or at play. If your morning doesn't provide a pleasant atmosphere, it's time to think about ways to create a positive start to the day.

Preschool Routines

Preschools are set up with a nice routine of the day that children can follow and understand. Schedules vary depending on the length of day. Generally preschool schedules include a circle or meeting time, free-play time, snack time, story time, and music time. Full day schools will include lunch and nap or quiet time.

Outdoor time should be a part of your child's daily routine, unless your preschool is in a city where accessibility to a safe outdoor play-area or park is not workable. You can find more information about the benefits of outdoor play in Chapter 5, *What Is Developmentally Appropriate?*

Having a routine during the school day is important for everyone. For children who find it difficult to make transitions, the preschool experience can be invaluable. In preschool, teachers have the time to help children transition to the next activity. They can give children the tools they need to transition on their own.

Preschools have to meet the needs of many children simultaneously. It may differ from what you feel is the ideal schedule for your child, but experienced teachers know how to make the day work for the group. They usually alternate lively play and free choice with quieter more directed times. The scheduling is intentional so children don't get overwhelmed. We don't want anyone to feel left out if they haven't mastered the skills to engage with the other children just yet.

Fear and frustration result for all of us when our expectations are not met. **For young children, there can be a significant amount of stress in not knowing what will be expected of them during the day.** Children depend on others dictating their day.

Some parents, concerned that children don't have enough say, allow young children to make family decisions and then wonder why the child is emotional or upset. "Why is Issam having such a bad day when he chose his bedtime, or he chose not to go to school today?" Imagine being 3- or 4-years-old and being responsible for yourself or the whole family. Even though your child might think he wants that choice, the stress of that level of responsibility is too much for a 4-year-old.

Thoughtful choices are necessary to build skills and confidence within a family framework. That framework needs to be established by the adults in the family so a child can feel secure.

Security at home allows your child the freedom to explore his world, knowing he is safe, and that his parents are there to guide him.

Evening Routines

Now let's explore the end of the day. Evening routines, or as I like to call them, the joys of bedtime are just as important as morning routines. We all know it can be a joy, but it can also be a problem. A wide variety of evening routines can work. The question is not what your bedtime routine is, but **is everyone getting plenty of sleep**, including the parents?

If what you're doing is working for everyone in the house, then life is good! If you or your child are stressed at bedtime, or if you or your child are not getting regular sleep, then it is worth taking the time to build a better evening routine. Be patient. New routines rarely kick in overnight, but a week of consistency can make an amazing difference.

Parents often think they are being kind by letting the child determine where and when to sleep. It can be a little confusing for a child age 3 or 4, to feel like his parents aren't in charge. It can lead to both the child and parent feeling sleep deprived.

If you cannot get regular sleep, it is hard to be a good parent during the day. It can be a vicious cycle. You're too tired to follow your planned bedtime routine and so you may fall asleep in the child's bed or build up resentment at bedtime.

Perhaps you or your child become emotional at bedtime. Everyone has an off day, but if any of these things are happening regularly, it's time for a positive change. Many families find change is much easier than expected, but you have to plan.

Change doesn't just happen. You need to prepare in advance. Both parents have to agree. If one parent is not in agreement, no matter how well thought out your fresh approach is, it may well be sabotaged which can be worse than not trying at all.

Experts will give you several steps and varied approaches to evening routines. I have listed a couple of resources at the end of the chapter and parentingscience.com has a section on sleep studies and helpful information under *preschoolers*. Take the time to find out why your child is having sleep difficulty. Could it be fears? Overstimulation? Just being over tired? The cause may well be a lack of a regular evening routine. Figuring out what the most likely cause is can save you a lot of time and frustration.

When my second child was born, my 4-year-old daughter wanted my attention at bedtime. She wanted me to stay with her after reading our evening story and I knew I still had to deal with the baby (off and on all night) as well as get some rest myself. We worked out a deal where after the story, I would move onto the floor, sit and meditate or relax for about 15 minutes. She was happy I was there, and she almost always fell asleep quickly.

I had time to relax my mind and when I got up to leave, since I wasn't on the bed, it did not wake my daughter. I could continue my evening, feeling refreshed. It was a great solution for us and it worked well for everyone in the family.

Each parent/family situation is unique and sleep issues change from month to month, sometimes week to week. That is why you have to take time to figure out what you need from an evening schedule and what your child needs. Your child may be old enough to be involved in the solution as my daughter was, or you may just have to explain what is going to happen so your child will know what to expect.

Once you have decided on a family course of action, plan ahead regarding how you will react so you can stay calm during implementation.

Know in advance that you may get less sleep for the first few nights. If you hold your ground, it is not uncommon for everyone to be sleeping better within a week. This is a life gift for your child. **Learning to be comfy, secure, and able to get to sleep will be a skill that your child will use the rest of his life** and not even know he should thank you for it!

Weekly Routines

Extraordinary learning comes from routines. Routines can be fun and something to look forward to each day or week. Perhaps you have a weekly outing on Thursdays to the library. Maybe on Friday evenings you pull out a basket with the special musical instruments and everyone gets to play and sing favorite songs. Your family may enjoy hiking with friends on the weekends.

I know quite a few families who have game night or movie night every week. Whatever your family enjoys doing together can become a regular activity that everyone can look forward to and enjoy. These are the family times your children will remember.

Routines should not be static. They will need to be revised, as the abilities of young children are always changing. A good routine provides structure to your child's life.

Let's go back to our morning routine as an example of keeping routines fluid. It may be one parent sets the breakfast table while the other helps the child dress and then you all have breakfast. Just a month later, your child can dress himself and help set the table.

Reassessing routines is vital to avoid frustrating your child, and to continue developing independence and confidence. Reassess every few months to make sure your child can make real contributions to the family routine. You don't want to fall into old habits when your child is ready to take on new challenges.

Giving actual jobs to your child may mean you have to reconsider where you keep some things in the kitchen so your child can easily access the broom or plates on his own.

Music Helps with Transitions

Many families like to add music into their routines. Most preschools not only have a music time but also use little songs to get children's attention when they are transitioning to a new activity. Songs get a child's attention and help a child prepare for what is coming next.

Feeling awkward about singing? Pick a song you know, like *Row, Row, Row Your Boat*, and change the words.

> Time, time, time to eat.
> Come and sit for lunch.
> There's some salad and some stew.
> Come sit down and munch.

A song can be a nice way to wake up in the morning too. It can be as simple as singing,

> Good morning,
> Good morning,
> Good morning to you.

Use any tune you like, or make up something. Simple is best. Music cues can be particularly helpful for children who have difficulty with transitions, like when it's time to clean up, or time to leave the house.

Down time should be part of your routine.

It can take some practice but down time will be a benefit to you and your child. Children and adults need quiet time to process the day. A regular naptime or quiet time is important, but don't underestimate the value of short 10-minute periods built into your day. For example, after lunch, everyone has a few minutes of quiet time.

Some children are so scheduled they never have a moment to assimilate all they have learned. They may not have time to be creative. Preschoolers will amaze you with their own ideas and capabilities if allowed the time and creative resources. More about time and creativity can be found in Chapter 9.

Upset Routines

Now let's consider the opposite of following a routine. What happens when the routine is upset? Your child might be upset too. Remember, a child will follow your lead. **One of the great life skills a parent can give a child is learning how to be flexible and adaptive.** Life is full of surprises, and schedules will always get interrupted.

Some children are more sensitive to schedule changes than others, but you can help by setting a calm example. Children provide a way for us to improve ourselves for their sake, when we wouldn't do it for ourselves. Being able to handle changes in routine makes life better for everyone. It can also provide you with unexpected learning and play experiences.

A schedule change can be a good thing. The snow day means we can go sledding and have hot chocolate. Justin's mom had to cancel our play date today. Now you and I can work on the tree house, or bake, or go explore the hiking trail, or explore the backyard with a magnifying glass. When my children were young, I always kept a couple of fun ideas in mind and ready to go when needed.

Comfort comes from knowing what to expect. Routines give us that base, but life is full of surprises. One of the best lessons for parents and children is to learn to handle change-to learn to welcome it. Look forward to new challenges and surprises. An unexpected change in plans can be an excellent learning opportunity or just fun.

One day I was taking my 3-year-old daughter to her favorite little thrift shop. This trip was a part of our regular weekly routine, and she loved it. On this day, the store was closed. My daughter was not happy.

We could have just gone home and felt disappointed for the rest of the afternoon. Instead, we drove past the store and turned onto a road we hadn't been on before and found a small park. That park was added into our weekly routine.

Changes in routine don't always have a happy ending. One of my students had a tough time with routine changes. Our first field trip of the year was especially hard on him. He wanted to be in the school with the normal routine. He spent the entire trip with a teacher, often complaining, *This is not right!* The teacher comforted him and pointed out all the interesting things around them. After school he still told his parents the trip was *not right*, but he also mentioned how he liked the apple trees and the hiking trail in the woods.

When the next field trip came up, he said, *This is not right!* The teacher reminded him how much he liked the last trip and told him that on this trip he would see a fire truck. He agreed to go and stayed by her side, but not all the time. By the end of the year, he looked forward to field trips. He was always a little nervous, but he knew he could handle each new adventure.

A change in routine, whether it is a planned event or something unexpected, can be an experience that teaches a child he'll be okay even if something goes wrong. He can handle it.

Further Reading for Parents

Pantley, Elizabeth. *The No-Cry Sleep Solution for Toddlers and Preschoolers.* (McGraw-Hill, 2005).

Our Daily Routine with Toddlers and Preschoolers

http://childhood101.com/2013/10/routines-toddlers-preschoolers/

Books to share with your child

Beskow, Elsa. *Peter's Old House.* (Floris Books, 1990).

Meddaugh, Susan. *Cinderella's Rat.* (Houghton Mifflin Company, 1997).

Cornwall, Gaia. *Jabari Jumps.* (Candlewick, 2017).

de la Peña, Matt; pictures by Robinson, Christian. *Milo Imagines the World.* (G.P. Putnam's Sons, 2021)

3
WHAT TO LOOK FOR IN A PRESCHOOL
FINDING THE RIGHT FIT

Key Factors:

The first step in your child feeling comfortable at school is you feeling comfortable with the school.

Looking out for your child's best interest includes looking out for your best interest.

A preschool should provide learning through experimentation.

Just because it's a preschool there is no guarantee that the curriculum is age appropriate and child-centered.

Mixed age groups often allow children to take on different roles.

You are your child's first, best, and most remembered teacher.

Ask about the turnover rate of staff at the school.

An outdoor play area is very important for this age group.

Nothing replaces meeting the people who will take care of your child, visiting the school and observing the classes.

∽

Let's prioritize some basic things you should expect your child's preschool to provide. When making your choice for the right school, consider not only your child's needs but also your needs as a parent.

If you are not comfortable with the school, it doesn't matter how many people recommend it or how prestigious the school is. You need to know this will be a good place to leave your child. If this is your first child going off to school, the transition may be a little difficult for you in the beginning. But, the transition will go smoother if you are confident your child is in expert hands. **The first step in your child feeling comfortable at school is you feeling comfortable with the school.**

Depending on where you live, there can be many options for preschool. A good place to start your selection process is to discuss as a family what matters most to each of you about the school. Make a list of the things you want in a preschool. You can use it as a checklist when you visit or research schools.

The easiest place to start your search is online. At the very least, you should be able to get preliminary answers to the following questions:

- What of the kind of facilities does the school have?
- What are the qualifications of their teachers?
- How many students does each teacher work with?

- What types of activities do the children engage in on a typical day.?

If you know parents whose children attend the school, ask about their experience.

Making a list of what you believe is important in a school and doing some preliminary research about schools in your area will give you a way to narrow your selection process to schools that best match your expectations. This prep work will also help you develop some specific questions for staff and will guide you on what to look for when you visit a school.

Remember, your child is unique. A school that is a perfect fit for your friend's child and family may not match your criteria. You and your child should always be the context in which you consider any information about a school.

Parents often tell me they were guided by their intuition when it came down to making the final selection of a preschool. After doing their research and visiting potential schools, they pick the school that they believe will provide the best care and best learning experience for their child.

When parents describe the role of intuition in their decision-making process, I know they have taken the first step in making sure that their child will have a good preschool experience. Your child is more likely to feel comfortable at the school if *you* are confident that the school is the right one for your family.

As you go through the school selection process, it can be an emotional experience. You want to find the best care for your child. Be careful not to rule out a wonderful school because the initial visit to the school is an emotionally exhausting experience for you or your child.

It's all a balance. Be careful not to project your past school memories, whether positive or negative, onto the school. Think in advance about what your child's needs are.

A mother and son were touring the school where I teach. During their tour, a child at the school, Joel, had a complete meltdown. Joel's mom was out of town, and he was not sleeping well. That morning was when he had had enough and he let everyone know it, loudly.

I sat down with Joel. We relaxed, talked about what he needed and he decided to join in at the play dough table. Witnessing crying children at a preschool can be upsetting, but it should not turn you away from that school.

I said to the registrar that the tour probably didn't go too well. She replied that the mother was so pleased with how the situation was handled; she applied before leaving the school that morning. A lot goes on at a preschool; don't be surprised if you see some behavior you don't care for. What's important is how the staff handles problems and moves forward.

Think in advance of what your current needs are as a parent (not what you feel you missed out on as a child). With these thoughts in mind, let's look at a few questions that can help you narrow your search.

What level of involvement do you want?

Whether you choose a school where you drop off your child and leave; a school where you can volunteer; or a cooperative school where you are an assistant teacher a certain number of days a month, you are choosing a community for your child and yourself.

It's important to choose a community where you feel comfortable. Starting school is a big step. It's doubtful that you will like every detail of any school. Focus on the basics. Are you comfortable in the school? Do you like the people; teachers, directors, and other parents? Do the teachers or directors seem approachable?

Sometimes what your child needs can differ from what you need. It's possible to have parents who want the community of a cooperative school, while their child is someone that thrives away from her parents. Some children find a love of independence early and enjoy having their own experience, separate from their parents.

In a case like this, a family might choose something in-between a traditional drop-off school and a cooperative school as the best choice. The solution may be a school that allows a few volunteer opportunities.

If you are interested in being very involved with your child's preschool experience, don't let the fact that both parents work dissuade you from checking into preschool cooperatives.

You can check the national list of cooperative preschools at Preschools.coop. Not all cooperative preschools are members of this organization so check with local parent groups in your area. Many cooperatives have different levels of involvement and various ways for parents to contribute. Even schools that require parents to volunteer in the classroom may be workable, if one parent has a flexible schedule.

Cooperative preschools can be wonderful, but they are not for everyone. Lilly, a parent of a young child, told me she was not a good mother because she did not enroll her child in one of the cooperative schools in our town. Of course, her assessment, was not true.

Lilly knew she needed that time to get her home together and to recharge her energy. Understanding her own personal needs was a big part of what made Lilly a great mom. She knew her child was in an excellent school and well cared for. This gave her the peace of mind she needed to take care of everything she had to do during the day, allowing her to be happy and ready to parent when her child was at home. She made the perfect choice for her family. You just can't compare your family's needs to other families' situations.

Finances may limit your school choice.

Schools offer various forms of scholarships and some offer lowered tuition for volunteer time so don't rule out a school you like until you've checked out all the possibilities.

Don't rule out an inexpensive school until you've toured it. Many schools find ways to keep tuition rates down, including having parent volunteers. If a school is out of your price range, I recommend you don't put your family under unnecessary financial duress for preschool–you'll be paying college tuition soon enough.

Be sure to consider parental needs.

Many young families live quite a distance from family members who can help with childcare. If you know you need the time your child is in school because of your work schedule or perhaps it is the only break you have from parenting, then that fact should be one of the deciding factors in your school search. A parent that feels overworked or stressed because he or she has no down time creates an unhappy family. **Looking out for your child's best interest includes looking out for your best interest.**

What are your child's learning needs?

Does the school provide learning opportunities that allow a student to enter at one level and travel through various levels of learning? Is this a place where your child can question, grow, and try new things? The best way to assess this is by talking to parents and teachers at the school. For example, what happens if your child finishes a project early, or has difficulty with a project?

The school needs to provide flexibility based on an individual child's interests and needs. When you tour the school, do you notice projects, games, or toys that allow for both simple play and play that requires more than one step? In quality preschools, this concept is built into the basic curriculum.

If there is a daily project, can children do it at multiple levels? Are there child accessible shelves where the children can find materials to extend their projects beyond what is shown to them by the teacher? There should always be an adult near the project area to help any child who needs help to understand or complete a project.

Does the school have areas where children can explore on their own?

Most schools have a science station, with hands on manipulatives that can change throughout the year. One example would be having *squishy circuits* (the name given to using play dough as an electrical conduit). Teachers may show children the basics regarding how the circuits and electricity work when first introduced to *squishy circuits*.

After the initial demonstration, the station is open for exploratory play. It is through experimentation that children discover that the current only flows one way. If you turn the light around, the light goes off. If you push the two play dough balls together the light goes off. Children learn that electricity just like water chooses the easiest path.

As the play goes on, the discoveries continue. **A preschool needs to provide learning through experimentation.**

If you are not familiar with "squishy circuits" you can learn about this fun, safe way to introduce young children to circuits at https://www.makerspaces.com/squishy-circuits

This is the kind of hands-on experimentation that takes time and thoughtfulness. You want to see a balance of this type of opportunity, along with group play and socialization.

Electricity and "Squishy Circuits."

Exploration shouldn't be confined to the science area. Large building blocks are great for children to experiment with. A child will figure out that the base of a tower needs to be larger to provide stability. A pathway made with blocks and boards may be narrow and children will have to figure out how to negotiate walking on it. Will it be a one-way street? Will you have to wait to walk? Can everyone take turns?

Let's discuss preschool curriculum.

Is the curriculum age appropriate? The goal should be to meet the child at their level and give them fun ways to grow and learn, while focusing on social development. I have visited schools that are under pressure from state mandates and other sources to teach in ways that are not in the best interest of the preschoolers, and can actually cause learning delays for some children.

You cannot assume the curriculum is age appropriate and child centered just because it's a preschool. Some preschools push Kindergarten or even First-Grade curriculum at the preschool level. Schools do this to show how academically prepared the children will be when they enter elementary school. The school may try to meet unrealistic expectations for kindergarteners.

This strategy often backfires. A child who misses the chance to learn how to play and get along with others will find elementary school very challenging. Children are expected to have already developed many social skills by the time they enter kindergarten.

Using math worksheets is an example of having inappropriate curriculum materials. They are simply developmentally inappropriate. Instead, the school should provide hands-on counting and grouping experiences through manipulatives, games, and pretend play.

Sorting nature items, counting marbles, and estimation jars are examples of concrete learning that young children can understand and think back to as their math skills grow. We teach hands on geometry in preschool. If you are building with the magnetic tiles and you need another square, what are you going to do? Given a little time, a child can surmise that two triangles can form the needed square.

You may be thinking, *my child loves those little preschool work books with numbers.* If that is the case, then enjoy those books with your child. Some children are ready for those books and love to do them, which is great as long as it doesn't become a chore or start them on the road to hating math. At the preschool level, the focus is on the group. We still learn our pre-math skills and it's a lot of fun.

Let's say we have 10 stuffed cats in the play animal shelter and four children want to buy cats. How many can we sell to each customer? On paper, the problem is meaningless. At the play animal shelter, it's fun.

We solve the problem by handing each customer a cat, or maybe two cats each, and noting how many cats are left. These pre-math experiences are physical and connect to a game the children want to play. Children build social skills, math skills, and language skills, all at the same time.

Forcing handwriting in preschool is another example of inappropriate curriculum. Studies have shown that pushing children to write with a pencil before they have developed fine motor skills means that a different part of the brain, the part used for gross motor skills, may try to adapt to meet the challenge.

Later, as the child's fine motor skills are developing, it can become very difficult for the child to integrate the writing skills that were pushed too early. It's much harder for a child to relearn the writing skills with a different part of the brain than it is for parents and teachers to be patient and let the child learn the skills when she is ready.

Pushing fine motor skills in preschool can lead to avoidable problems with writing in first or second grade. Instead, a school should provide multiple ways to improve fine motor skills. Those paths include painting, sewing, coloring, playing instruments, manipulating puzzles, planting seeds, singing songs with hand motions, etc.

Instead of forcing writing on children who are not ready, a preschool should provide many ways for learning about letters, from viewing them and painting on a big easel to making signs for the play animal shelter. You can find more on what is age appropriate in Chapter 5.

If you would like an in depth understanding of how a child's brain grows and develops, be sure to check out the work of Jane Healy. She has done decades of research on brain development. I list one of her books as a resource at the end of this chapter.

Let's get back to preschool options.

How much variety and choice would you like for your child? Is the preschool in a single room? Do children have freedom of movement between rooms? If they limit the children to one classroom, is it set up with a wide variety of stations and activities? Do children have a choice of activities for a large part of the day?

Does the school or classroom have a quiet area? Whether it is a library or a resting place, children need a calm area. This is especially true if your child has sensory issues, but even the most enthusiastic, outgoing child needs a quiet place sometimes. We all need time to relax and take in what we've learned.

Are children separated by age or are there mixed age groups? Both settings can work well. **Mixed age groups often allow children to take on different roles.** One day your child might feel like leading a game, the next day your child may want to follow another child's lead, or play alone for a while.

These options are important and should be available in any group, but are often easier to access in a mixed age group of 3- to 5-year-olds. Preschool is about learning through social interactions. Social growth will be limited if your child plays with a tiny group of children who are all about the same age.

In small groups, social roles become quickly ingrained. Aisha always picks the game. Jackson always helps her set up. Sam always feels frustrated! Can Sam move to a group of younger children where he can lead an activity some days? He can still play with Aisha when he wants to play her game. Then Sam will continue to work on both leading and following. While we're at it, the teacher will want to watch for an opportunity for Jackson to lead the play as well.

Does the school strive for diversity of various kinds?

Depending on the school and the community, this can mean different things. Perhaps the school has scholarships to help provide socio-economic diversity. Are there families of different ethnicities at the school? Exposing children to different cultures and languages at an early age is a wonderful gift that opens up a child's world. It can be a significant experience for everyone in the family and a way to build a kinder world.

Schools cannot discriminate in order to diversify, so this may mean you are looking for a school in a community that is more diverse, or a school that addresses diversity in its curriculum. Many schools have guest speakers throughout the year. Some schools make it a priority to meet with other schools occasionally. A community playground can be a perfect setting for a meetup.

Age diversity may mean the school also has a kindergarten or a daycare. If the school facility includes a daycare, make sure there are appropriate activities and manipulatives to engage and challenge your preschooler when the more formal learning activities are not going on. The preschool needs to expand your child's horizons.

Is the preschool meeting the most basic needs?

The most important lessons to learn in preschool are how to work and play with others. This requires a great deal from a child, including language skills, empathy, and creative problem solving. "How can we all get a turn?" Many of these skills become more difficult to teach the older a child gets. Social skills are profoundly important for each child's future school career and confidence.

I mentioned the inappropriateness of worksheets for this age. Children can do worksheets, but why? We can easily incorporate many pre-math and pre-writing skills into play with other children.

Learning through play is a deeper learning experience and is much more meaningful to a child. That's why you send your child to a professional preschool teacher who knows how to turn playing pirates into a game. A game that incorporates social cooperation, labeling and map reading skills, not to mention inventory of the booty. Avast ye!

Experienced teachers are aware of the difficulties that arise when schools push material that is above a child's cognitive level. They also know the importance of making sure that a child who is ready to move on can. The next chapter will give you an idea of the variety of curricula available and the need for that variety.

Should you consider location and tuition costs?

Some parents, while searching for the perfect school, will find a place that requires a long commute or perhaps a stressful drop-off/pick-up schedule. I mention this because a calm, happy family is one of the best gifts you can give your child.

Trying to get a child to a school that is too expensive or so far away that it causes stress for the parents is generally ill-advised, even if it appears to be the perfect school. After all, **you are your child's first, best, and most remembered teacher.**

If you are stressed and under pressure all the time, the few hours in school are not enough of a consolation for your child to compensate for the stress she may sense at home.

I have known several families who drove long distances for their children to attend preschools they thought were the best.

In some of those cases, as the year went on, their child missed more and more school days. It was just too difficult for the families to keep up the schedule. It was stressful on the parents and hard on the children who wanted to play with their friends. Try not to make your life too difficult. Sometimes it is best to be practical. If there is a good school nearby, more time with your child and less time in the car is the best option.

What is the best size for a preschool?

Ideally, a small school or small class grouping within a larger school is best for preschoolers. Some large schools have great programs, but can be overwhelming for a 3-year-old.

I have seen large schools that have found excellent ways to divide their spaces, making it less intimidating for young children. One school added a small house on the property when growing rather than expanding the existing building to deal with a growing population at the preschool. The new preschool classes were in their own little comfy house.

I can't give you an exact number for the perfect class or school size because it's more a matter of your child feeling comfortable in the space. Too few children and your child's social growth could be limited. You might need to supplement it. Too many children or too large a building and your child can feel overwhelmed.

Concerned about the school's staff?

Ask about the turnover rate of staff at the school. Preschoolers thrive on a solid base from which they can explore new things. All schools hire new teachers and assistants from time to time, but if the school constantly must hire new teachers, be sure to ask why this is the case. Inexperienced staff can add energy to a program, but experienced staff members are a must for maintaining continuity and quality in any program.

Ask about outdoor time.

Having an outdoor play area is very important for this age group. I wouldn't write off an excellent school just because the facility does not allow for a playground. Some schools just don't have outdoor facilities but they will make use of local parks and nature areas.

City schools can have an extra challenge in this area. Do the teachers bring nature items into the school? Have they met the physical needs of this age group? Is there an indoor area with climbers and slides? Teachers of this age group know physical play, especially gross motor skill development, is a must. Those skills are the first step as the children move on to cooperative games, confidence building, overcoming fears, and developing fine motor skills.

Every state has special rules for playground and indoor climber safety. You want to notice and ask if the structures are regularly assessed and maintained. All outdoor structures should be surrounded by several feet of open space in case a child falls.

It is best if there are a variety of types of play structures. Swings are nice for individual play, but a place to play pretend house or a big climber allows for group play as well. Outdoor areas for community games like chase or working in the mud kitchen allow for social and physical growth. Natural areas also work well for young children.

Whether your child will play indoors or outside, nothing is a substitution for good supervision.

How can you make a judgment about how safe your child will be in this school?

This is all about competence. Competence is found in experienced and respected staff members. Check the turnover rate at the school. New, enthusiastic teachers can be wonderful assets for a school, but a lack of experienced staff can be a problem. You want to make sure an adult with experience is monitoring things.

Check with your state social services or education department to find out about the school's licensure and infraction record. Many states have so many guidelines that most schools have a few infractions, but you want to know if there are serious or recurring safety infractions.

As useful as this information is, **nothing replaces meeting the people who will take care of your child, visiting the school and observing the classes.** Competent preschool directors want you to come for a tour to make sure the school is a good fit for your child.

Picking a school is like picking a life partner. Pick one you already like, don't plan on being able to change the situation. You can add your family to the community and your ideas to the school, but don't expect to change a school into a different place.

Some schools allow for a great deal of parent involvement, you may introduce some new ideas or practices–but you will not make it into a different school, and no school can meet every parent's desires. You need to find a place where you feel comfortable with the school's general practices.

What do you do if you can't find your dream preschool, but you feel your child is ready to learn with other children? Prioritize what you and your child need verses what you would like. Often when we worry about our child's well-being, it's easy to get hung up on some of the minor details and miss the bigger picture.

Safety and staff experience should be near the top of the list. Make sure you're not ruling out a suitable school because of something that has little to do with the quality of the school, staff, or your child's well-being.

One parent was considering leaving a school because she was uncomfortable with the idea of field trips and having her child leave the school without her. As a first-time parent, it can be hard enough to send a child to preschool; but if you are a worrier, it is even more difficult to think of that child going somewhere else without you. Here, the parent expressed her fear to the teachers.

It's all about communication. She could have kept her child home on a field trip day, but there's no growth in that for child or parent. The teacher recommended that the parent join the class on the field trip. The teacher knew that no amount of explaining safety procedures would help a parent who was already fearful.

Two little outings later, and the parent was no longer worried. She became a promoter of the trips once she saw how they worked, and once she saw how much her child enjoyed them.

It can be harder for you to let go than it is for your child to go off on her own adventure. A good preschool staff will help you work through these types of problems, but you have to communicate with them. After all, the school staff members are used to running the school (and in this case field trips). The trips are just a regular part of the job for the teachers. They may not realize you are uneasy. Be clear in your communication.

If the best-fit preschool you have found is missing some elements you would like in a school, are they things you can supplement at home? If there is not enough physical activity, you can sign up for a tumbling class or have a regular play date at the park.

You can supplement hands-on and exploratory learning experiences by allowing your child to help you with real tasks at home. Helping in the kitchen can be a great learning opportunity, especially when you talk with your child as you work together. As we discussed in Chapter 1, household chores are a great way for a child to learn.

The one thing many of us can't do or don't have the time or means to supplement at home is plenty of socialization with peers. Children learn a lot more from their peers than they do from adults. You may always share the doll with your child, but another child expects his turn and expects it *now*. If your child needs more socialization opportunities, you will need to arrange for your child to have playtime with other children outside the school environment.

Applications

Many schools require applications very early, sometimes a year or more in advance. Don't let that fact cause undue stress. Most communities have a variety of preschool options. Check with local schools and see when most schools accept applications for the next year.

If you are not ready by that time or are moving to a new community right before the new school year, you are not alone. Because young families often move in the summer, many schools end up with openings right at the beginning of the school year even if they told you they were full at the beginning of the summer. If you're in a situation like this, get on the waiting list for a couple schools and stay in touch with them.

Attending a preschool that is a good fit for your family is a big adventure for your child. Change and growth come with joy and growing pains. Preschool is a big step into the wider world. A little time touring a few schools will pay off in finding the right fit for your family.

What About Home-Based Preschools?

This can be tricky. I know several wonderful teachers who run great small preschools out of their homes. I would not hesitate to recommend them, but I know those teachers and I have seen them with children. Some of the best teachers I know run their own small in-home schools.

Many home-based schools are licensed, but in most states, they are not required to be licensed if they only take in a few children. Every state has different requirements. Remember, licensure doesn't consider the quality of the curriculum.

Checking with your state can tell you if a licensed program has health and safety violations. Statistics show that more serious accidents happen in home preschool settings than in formal preschools.

The answer here is simple. Meet the teacher. Ask for references and talk to them. Use your judgement and knowledge of your child's needs. Above all, visit the school.

Children using pine needle paint brushes.
Schuylkill Center Nature Preschool, PA Photo
Credit: Kristina Eaddy

Investigating soil during exploration time at
Schuylkill Center Nature Preschool, PA Photo
Credit: Nicole Brin

Further Reading for Parents

Healy, Jane M. *Your Child's Growing Mind: A Practical Guide to Brain Development and Learning from Birth to Adolescence.* (Broadway Books, 2004).

Choosing a Preschool or Childcare Center

http://www.pbs.org/parents/education/going-to-school/choosing/preschool

4

SPECIFIC CURRICULA

Many teachers will tell you that their preferred curriculum is the best one for all children. My belief that there is no one best curriculum for all preschoolers. There are too many variables. Some excellent preschools use their own curriculum, which has been developed over years. Others use a variety of approaches depending on the current teachers and the philosophy of the school.

I will not be covering curriculum for special needs children; you can ask questions of teachers at any school that interests you. More and more communities have programs for children who need a specialized preschool or extra help. It is best to check with your local school system for referrals.

This chapter covers a few of the most popular curricula. I have included national websites, but a visit to your local school to see the curriculum being taught is important. Any curriculum is only as good as the teachers and school implementing it.

I want to mention a couple terms you are likely to hear from those involved in preschool education. First up, is *play-*

based. In a *play-based* curriculum, learning is embedded in play and the teachers are trained to follow the child's lead.

Play-based doesn't mean the teachers are just watching children play. Professional teachers are trained in helping children work with others and solve problems together. They introduce academic concepts through imaginative games and play.

If a school tells you they have a *play-based* curriculum, it's a good sign. It is also a fun, age-appropriate way to weave pre-math and pre-reading skills into preschool's most important job, which is developing social skills.

The other term to listen for is *inquiry-based*. Powerful programs ask questions and follow the child's lead. Teachers will ask questions to figure out what a child knows about a topic.

Here is a simple example; a teacher shows the children a pinecone and asks what they think about it without explaining or correcting the children's ideas. Next, the teacher can follow up by taking a walk where children can observe pine trees. Later a basket or nature table at school may have various pine needles, pinecones, and bark for touching and sorting.

It takes practice for adults to step back and let children learn and discover. *Inquiry-based* learning uses questions to discover what children know and sometimes to give them ideas to explore. What it doesn't do is tell or lecture the children. We want to encourage creative thinking and children's natural curiosity.

You can have a wonderful preschool with well-trained supportive staff that borrow from various teaching philosophies to make a strong learning environment. You can also have a school that follows a quality curriculum, but the curriculum is taught by under trained or unhappy staff members. That isn't good for anyone. Be sure to visit the individual preschool.

The Creative Curriculum

The *Creative Curriculum* is used by many schools. Any school can purchase and use this curriculum. It has been around for decades. The curriculum has 38 researched based objectives and leads teachers (and therefore children) through everything from language usage to regulating emotions and behavior. It provides great support to teachers.

This is a solid curriculum that is particularly helpful to newer teachers and schools. It is often used in Head Start programs as it relies on assessments and guidelines that bring consistency to a program. For more information about the Creative Curriculum: https://teachingstrategies.com/solutions/teach/preschool

Montessori

Many families choose *Montessori* schools. This curriculum often provides specific types of helpful guidance. Are transitions difficult for your child? Perhaps your child can't function well without clear boundaries, but you still want your child to have creative opportunities. A Montessori school may be a good choice for your child.

Maria Montessori stressed freedom within limits, allowing children to work uninterrupted for long periods of time, while also learning their place in the group. Montessori Schools are set up to provide both order and personal responsibility. They provide freedom of choice within a prepared environment. Learn more at the National Montessori Association:

https://amshq.org

Reggio Emilia

You may have heard of the *Reggio Emilia* approach. Local parents and Loris Malaguzzi, who was a teacher near Reggio Emilia, Italy, after World War II, created this curriculum. It is an arts and community based approach that starts with the concept that each child is competent and capable. A high priority is placed on the ascetics of the school.

When a topic of study is chosen teachers and parents will ask questions to figure out what the children already know. Then teachers provide further elements for children to discover. The goal is to provide a self-guided curriculum for children, to the extent possible. It is a curriculum designed to allow children to explore the world around them in a supportive environment, which is carefully set up emphasizing beauty and natural materials.

https://www.reggioalliance.org

Waldorf

Waldorf education includes rituals which can provide balance in a child's life. Waldorf schools help children explore the world with a sense of wonder. The arts play an important role in creative exploration. Waldorf teachers really take their time with preschoolers. Instead of telling a story once, it may be told for many days in different ways, and include the use of puppets or dolls. Repetition is so important for young children and often ignored by adults who are ready to move on to the next activity.

Natural items are a large part of the preschool classroom as the children move through the seasons of the year. In the early school years traditional academics are de-emphasized. The arts, storytelling and practical skills are accentuated. https://www.waldorfeducation.org

Photo Credit: ***Our Neighborhood Child Development Center***, Charlottesville, VA. Inquiry-based learning.

Photo Credit: ***Our Neighborhood Child Development Center***, Charlottesville, VA. Reggio inspired school.

Nature and Outdoor Schools

Nature Preschools and Nature-based Preschools are a growing trend in the United States. There have always been nature-based preschools, but parents and teachers are expanding the opportunities for outdoor learning across the country.

What do these schools have in common? Outdoor preschools are almost always *play-based* and *inquiry-based*. They may or may not follow a specific curriculum, though many nature preschools use the Reggio approach for inquiry and developmental documentation. Some schools borrow their pedagogy from the German forest schools or waldkindergartens, where children spend the entire day outside.

As more and more children and adults spend less time in nature, these programs cover all the preschool basics while immersing children in the great outdoors. Children learn to appreciate and enjoy the world around them. Children, and hopefully parents, develop a comfort level and confidence which will lead them to not only spend more time outside but also to appreciate the need to care for our natural areas and all the plants and creatures who live there.

Around cities, many nature centers have added Nature Preschools. If you are looking for something with more outdoor time and nature focus, checking in with your local nature center is a good place to start. You can also find schools in your area at the North American Association for Environmental Education, or NAAEE at:

http://naturalstart.org

Many wonderful preschools find ways to bring the great outdoors inside and even traditional preschools often go outside every day. We will cover the importance of including the outdoors in early childhood development in Chapter 5, *What is Developmentally Appropriate?*

It cannot be stressed enough that the effectiveness of any curricula in practice depends on the particular staff. Several of the programs mentioned in this chapter have curriculum that is based on the work of a single person who is now deceased. Over the years the programs of study have grown and changed, but all are well tested and have many benefits.

A caring professional staff and a curriculum that allows for exploration, curiosity, and social interaction are the most important elements of any preschool.

Sliding in the mud. There's no such thing as bad weather; if you have the right clothes! ***Dodge Nature Preschool***, West St. Paul, MN.

Tracking animal prints in the snow at ***Dodge Nature Preschool***, West St. Paul, MN

Wide-open spaces are an invitation to run and play. ***The Nature Preschool at Irvine***, Owings Mills, MD.

An outdoor classroom at ***The Nature Preschool at Irvine***, Owings Mills, MD.

Further Reading for Parents

Britton, Lesley. *Montessori Play and Learn: A Parent's Guide to Purposeful Play from Two to Six.* (Crown Publishers Inc., 1992).

Curtis, Deb and Carter, Margie, *Designs for Living and Learning: Transforming Early Childhood Environments.* (Redleaf Press, 2014).

Edwards, Carolyn; Gandini, Lella; Forman, George; Editors. *The Hundred Languages of Children: The Reggio Emilia Approach – Advanced Reflections.* (Ablex Publishing Corporation, 1998).

Oppenheimer, Sharifa. *Heaven on Earth: A Handbook for Parents of Young Children.* (Steiner Books, 2006).

Petrash, Jack. *Understanding Waldorf Education: Teaching from the Inside Out.* (Gryphon House, 2002).

5

WHAT IS DEVELOPMENTALLY APPROPRIATE?

Key Factors:

Open-ended projects are an essential element of a developmentally appropriate preschool.

If you enter a preschool and see rows of bright, colorful projects that all look neat and alike, this is a red flag.

Every child develops at their own pace in a developmentally appropriate preschool.

One of the great things about preschool, particularly if this is your first child, is that you get the chance to see your child interact with and among peers.

Professional preschool teachers will contact you for a meeting if there is a concern. If that happens, remember this is a good thing.

Early intervention can often be easy and make a huge difference for your child.

It is best to keep young children away from television and specifically from television news.

As your child grows, he will experience times when he needs extra sleep and times when he just can't sleep. This is normal.

What kind of life would your parents have wanted for you?

Having too many things is overwhelming.

Parents often work too hard and spend too much money on a party that no one enjoys.

For your child, the gift of your time is better than any toy.

Educators and parents alike discuss and praise the virtues of a preschool program being developmentally appropriate. It would be hard to find a preschool that wasn't described by its promoters as developmentally appropriate. Even though some schools are clearly not what most educators would consider on target for 3- to 5-year-olds. How can you find the right level for your child? It's all about listening to people in the school community and, if possible, visiting the school.

Open-ended projects are an essential element of a developmentally appropriate preschool. Projects should allow for different interpretations and skill levels. Professional teachers have training and experience to allow them to gauge development in many areas of learning, to include motor, language, social, and cognitive skills. They are familiar with learning patterns in children.

No two children develop all these skills at the same age. So, being developmentally appropriate is all about flexibility and observation. Look for open-ended toys. Lincoln Logs are fun, but they are designed to be put together in specific ways. In contrast, building block sets of various sizes can be made into anything your child imagines.

If you enter a preschool and see rows of bright, colorful projects that all look neat and alike, this is a red flag. It is a sign that the teachers did most of the work. Most schools do pre-cut or prepared projects occasionally, but if cookie cutter projects appear to be the norm at a school, it's a sign that the program is not developmentally appropriate.

Here are some reasons you might find these types of projects at a preschool:

1. The teachers or administrators are in a competitive school environment. They believe more parents who are looking for a quality preschool will enroll their child if it looks like the children's work is of a *higher* quality. These pre-cut projects are only thought of as higher quality by people who are unfamiliar with what quality preschool work looks like.

2. The school may have inexperienced staff. They may put the physical appearance of the finished product over the importance of the process and allowing children to experiment. These teachers do not understand and appreciate what hands-on preschool learning looks like. They do not realize that creative exploration is how children will develop the skills the teachers are trying to encourage.

3. It can be a sign that a teacher is too controlling and does not allow children to explore materials or follow their own creative instincts. There certainly are times when a teacher is hoping to focus on a specific task, but if all

creative projects are micromanaged, they are no longer creative.

~

How can you tell if the school is meeting the needs of the children? Talking to parents and teachers is helpful; a visit to the school is the best way to see if children are engaged in their activities. Are they interested in what they are learning, and generally happy? I say generally happy, because with preschoolers it is not uncommon for someone to have a bad day and show it. You want to observe the big picture.

Although it is hard to define what exact activities are developmentally appropriate for any one age group, you can find a list of norms for children grouped by ages, which can give you an idea of what to expect as your child grows.

The CDC has a very detailed list at: https://www.cdc.gov/ncbddd/actearly/milestones

3-year-old norms...

Some of these tasks require help at first. Three-year-olds are able to be quite independent. They can be asked to put on and take off their own clothing (even get it out of a drawer and put it in the hamper). They should be able to help you with simple tasks at home like sweeping (a small broom helps), dusting, and setting the table.

At school we would expect them to use the toilet and wash their hands on their own (some may need a little coaching at first). They should be able to actively listen and contribute for a few minutes at circle time. They handle hands-on projects. Three-year-olds may still play independently, they generally start to play next to a friend (parallel play).

4-year-old norms...

Now they are really ready to help out. Confidence and self-reliance are built by having real chores at home. Many children at this age can choose their own outfits and dress themselves.

At school we start to see children engaging more with their peers when playing. They understand simple group games, puzzles, and running games. They think a lot and can have some difficulty navigating play when others don't follow the rules. This is great practice for learning to work and play with others. Be careful not to over or under praise their arts and crafts. Instead, you can try to follow their enthusiasm and point out interesting details.

5-year-old norms....

This is when we really expect to see some independence and the "I can do it myself" attitude. If you actually want something done, be careful not to leave too many options open. For example, "Should we clean your room now or after lunch?" is a much better question than "When should we clean your room?" (That particular example is true for teenagers too.)

Five-year-olds are usually very excited to show off their new physical skills. There need to be opportunities at home and at school for running, jumping, climbing, kicking, and tossing a ball. Many children are ready for casual group sports.

Every child develops at their own pace in a developmentally appropriate preschool. There is a typical sequence of development, and general skills that show up around a certain age, but the range of normal is vast.

Some developments are hard on parents. Lying generally starts between the ages of 3 and 5. It's an important moment in brain development and means your child now understands that each person thinks differently. Though it is usually nothing to worry about, we will cover it in Chapter 7, *Worries and Fears*.

There are many excellent books regarding how the brain works and the sequence of brain development from a scientific perspective. Dr. Jane Healy's classic, *Your Child's Growing Mind,* and Daniel J. Siegel, Tina Payne Bryson's, *The Whole-Brain Child: 12 Revolutionary Strategies to Nurture Your Child's Developing Mind, Survive Everyday Parenting Struggles, and Help Your Family Thrive,* are both listed at the end of the chapter.

These books are helpful in understanding what's going on as your child's brain grows. They can give you an idea of what to expect sequentially.

Now for some practical learning from the classroom. **One of the great things about preschool, particularly if this is your first child, is that you get the chance to see your child interact with and among peers.**

This is particularly true if your child is at a cooperative preschool or a school that expects you to volunteer, as many Reggio programs do. You will get a feel for where most children are with motor skills, language skills, and social skills.

Noticing the norm is useful. Comparing every individual skill can be harmful for you and your child.

I recall a parent sitting with her child. Her child was just learning to use scissors and was next to a boy who was almost a full year older, and was a very experienced scissor user. The mother became concerned and was noticeably frustrated with her child's scissor skills. This type of direct child-to-child comparison helps no one and can be counterproductive. It's frustrating for both child and parent.

A preschool teacher takes each child where he is skill-wise when he enters the school and goes from there. This classroom had ample and varied manipulatives to help this child develop fine motor skills, so it was just a matter of a little time before he was on his way to cutting paper with ease.

If you have a specific concern about your child's development in an area, set up a meeting with the teacher. There may be some fun ways to continue to develop those skills at home.

All children grow at different speeds and have natural abilities in some areas and not others. You don't want to worry because Rosa can handle those scissors like a professional and Jamal can barely hold them. Jamal already pumps on the swing and Rosa hasn't figured that out yet. Beyond individual differences, there are age and gender differences. In just a few months, young children can make enormous strides in learning new skills.

Your child's teacher should notice various traits in your child, and whether they are inside or outside of the wide range, they see on a daily/yearly basis. **Professional preschool teachers will contact you for a meeting if there**

is a concern. If that happens, remember this is a good thing.

The teacher has your child's best interest at heart and just wants to make you aware of the concern. Your child's teacher can give you some ideas or professional contacts (if needed) to help your child feel confident and capable.

Many parents want their child to be the best at some skills at school. I cannot emphasize this enough; *A preschool teacher works with a child at whatever stage the child is at when entering the school and goes forward from that point.*

Preschool teachers view learning is an individual experience, not a competitive one. There are just too many variables to make direct comparisons on skill sets useful. Noticing where each child is, and helping them to grow socially, verbally, cognitively, and with motor skills is the priority.

If you are watching your child in school, you need to know that many children act differently when a parent is in the room. If you see behavior that concerns you, be sure to ask the teacher if that is how your child behaves when you aren't there.

There are certain matters preschool teachers will note because **early intervention can often be easy and make a huge difference for your child.**

It's hard to hear that your child's teacher has a concern about a developmental issue, but it is important to listen. It's difficult not to be upset or emotionally invested. Like you, your child's teacher wants what's best for your child. It would be more upsetting if there was something like a speech problem keeping your child from being understood by playmates and the teacher said nothing.

Maybe it's something that can clear up with the help of a specialist. What if no action was taken to intervene and help your child? Although many preschool teachers have specialties, most are not specialists in speech pathology or various therapies.

Teachers do work with these specialists, and it is the teacher's job to let you know if a specialist would be helpful. A language specialist, for example, can tell you if a certain speech pattern is something not to worry about because it is quickly out grown; if it is something that a few months of practice can correct; or if there is a real problem.

Clear communication and the right person for the job give you peace of mind and the best outcome for your child. You may have questions about a behavior that troubles you. If you have a specific concern, let the teacher know as soon as possible.

Teachers may notice when a child has sensory issues (auditory or tactile, for example). It's important to note these concerns and share them with you. Some can be signs of other issues, from lack of hearing to physical difficulties that can often be resolved at a young age with professional intervention.

If your child is experiencing some difficulty, many specialists and parents find a comfort in labels. If there is an issue, you need to acknowledge that situation and have some idea of what it is, so you can make a plan. Other parents have a deep fear of labeling any attribute of their child, concerned it will cause people to see their child negatively.

The middle road is best. If we (parents, teachers, and specialists) are working together, we can't fear words. Accurately describing your child's concern may require labeling it. It's important to differentiate various issues, for example, sensory issues from autism.

We're working with preschoolers, so we have to be prepared for things to be in flux. Don't waste time worrying about semantics. Focus on your child and giving them time to discover who they are and what they can do. A label doesn't stop you from focusing on your child, noticing what they take interest in, and moving forward together.

We have gone over appropriate practices at school, but most of your child's time is spent outside of school. Here are some best practices for the preschool age group.

We all know it - minimal television or screen time is best for young children. In reality, it's all around us but it's never as good as a person, a classic toy, or an art box. **It is best to keep young children away from television and specifically from television news.**

It's surprising what children pick up, with the current sensationalized media. Adults get fired up too about things that are happening far away, or even stories that are misreported. I'm all for staying informed, but everything has a time and place. A home with preschoolers is a home that needs to have parents in the present and engaged in their family's world, listening and learning with your children.

The over sensationalized, scary opinion/news programs will strive to convince all viewers that their very life depends on staying glued to the television. That is the job of their marketers. As parents and teachers, our jobs require focus on our children in the present. Limiting media is an empowering choice for the entire family. To quote one of my favorite family singer-songwriters, Ken Lonnquist, *"TV stands for Time Vacuum"*. Be mindful of your program preferences for your family.

The reality for most of us is that you and your family will enjoy your favorite shows and sometimes children will over hear the news or discussion of a stressful subject on the television and have questions. Children often take things literally. Adults who use super hyperbole to describe situations, and reporters who over dramatize the news, can affect children.

During a presidential campaign years ago, two of my students were arguing as we waited for everyone's parents to pick them up.

> Suddenly I heard a loud, *I hate candidate X!*
>
> Followed by, *I want to kill candidate Y!*
>
> I approached the children and said, *Let's take a deep breath. Do you know candidate X or candidate Y?*
>
> They both replied with a quiet, *No.*
>
> We discussed how these are people with families who love them. Both candidates had children and one candidate had grandchildren who were preschool age.
>
> *I didn't know that*, said one child while calming down.
>
> The other child said, *Well, I hate his ideas.*

This was not a discussion I was planning to have with preschoolers, but now we could talk. I could reply disagreeing with someone's ideas is okay. In fact, it's why we have elections so people can vote and choose between candidates who have different ideas.

Children hear what you say, even when you think a child is busy at play and not paying attention. Parents are often infallible in the eyes of their children. If you want to teach reason, logic, or calmness, practice those skills yourself.

It's important not to talk down to children, but there is no need to worry your child with abstract fears they cannot do anything about. Children don't need adult burdens. They have enough to think about. These are topics for parents.

A brief word on sleep, which is covered more in chapters 2 and 7. Sleep is critical for your child's growth and development. **As your child grows, he will experience times when he needs extra sleep and times when he just can't sleep. This is normal.**

Preschoolers' bodies and brains are growing at a rapid rate and need adequate rest. Finding a bedtime routine that allows you and your child to get adequate sleep most of the time will solve and prevent many problems.

In a perfect world we all hope to set a calm, happy example. It's harder some days than others, but children learn most from watching you, their parent and greatest teacher. The best way to raise a calm, happy, and fulfilled child is by being a calm, happy, and fulfilled adult. It's easy to say, "Be sure to take care of yourself." It's harder to do, as the demands of work, family, and life can be overwhelming at times.

If you find yourself so busy with the kids that you never feel you can take a moment for yourself, think about the following question. What do you want for your child's life? Do you want your child to forego all dreams and aspirations? Do you want your child to feel that the only right thing to do is take care of others all the time and sacrifice self-happiness?

Your child will learn from your example. **What kind of life would your parents have wanted for you?** Even during the preschool years, you should continue with something that brings you joy. It may or may not be something you can enjoy with your child, but it is important for children to see a parent as a separate person with unique interests.

We often live what we learn as children. If you want your children to have happy, healthy, balanced lives, then you need to strive to have a happy, healthy, balanced life. That doesn't mean shirking your parental responsibilities. A self-absorbed parent is as bad an example as those who give away all their self-worth to someone else. Find the balance that works for your family. It will vary over the years as family demands change.

Some days we are short on sleep and tested in public by a child who may be equally exhausted. Every parent wants to care for their child to the best of their ability. To do this, you must remember to take care of yourself. It's easy to have high expectations, but give yourself the same permission you give your child to learn new things and to fail. That's how we all learn and grow.

A few words on stuff! Things get in the way of life. Before you bring new things into your child's world, be sure that the item in question enhances life and has a purpose.

The purpose can be as simple as the item is beautiful, or it makes you smile. What you need to know is that for a child (and for many adults), **having too many things is overwhelming.** Things can block creativity and impede you living your life.

Start a clean-out routine while your child is young. When a new toy comes into the house, is there an old one that is no longer played with that can be given away? You won't do a clean out every time something new comes into the house, but if you start it as a routine, I guarantee it will improve your future life.

Creating a simpler, more comfortable home environment will encourage your child to be less obsessed with things. Sometimes taking a picture of a once loved toy can make it easier to keep the memory and let go of the toy. It also helps to explain to your child that the toy will go to a thrift store, where it can make another child happy. Now your child has room for his new toy.

The preschool years are a great time to start family traditions. It's fun to have events that everyone in the family can contribute to. Maybe everyone reads, or tells a favorite story or poem on a holiday.

Be thoughtful about what traditions you start. Do you like staying up late preparing for some special event every year? Are you a morning person? I got a little tired of having to get up early on birthday mornings to prepare breakfast in bed as we entered the teen years, but I would do it again.

As for that clean out tradition, twice a year works great. Get rid of things you and your child no longer need, want, or use. Have several boxes: things to keep, donate, or trash, and a box for things that are no longer played with but are hard to give up. Put the box away. If no one looks for the item for 6 months to a year, it's donated.

It helps if you can donate items to a place your child knows. It could be a school or a thrift shop. You and your child may know a family with younger children or perhaps a daycare that could use the items. Most children are happier to give something away if they know it's going to a suitable home.

Perhaps you set your clean up times a couple weeks before birthdays or holidays because you need to make room for new toys. It can be easier to part with toys if new ones are on the way.

Toys aren't the only things that can pile up. One problem parents of preschoolers often face is what to do with all those school projects and works of art? If you start good habits regarding these treasures early, you will be much happier in the long run.

Can your child's paintings be used as wrapping paper? We all save a few, but if you have many pieces of art can you take a picture of them and preserve the memory that way? Some schools have woodworking areas that are great for confidence building. It takes a lot of practice to learn to drill, hammer, and build. This means you could end up with many little pieces of wood entering the house. I have seen families put the projects together to make a sculpture and take a picture, before recycling the wood. Other parents have a little shelf and say, "6 pieces of art or woodworking can go here." Your child can keep an old favorite and still add in recent works, but some have to go.

Birthday parties often start with preschoolers and gifts are expected. You can always give a fun game or outdoor toy. These are things to be shared. I once saw a family bring a child his favorite pie for a birthday present. The birthday child was elated. Everyone enjoyed eating the pie. A great memory was made, and thankful parents had one less plastic toy in the house.

Birthdays can be challenging for reasons other than getting too many things. Large parties can overwhelm young children. A smaller family event or a gathering of a few friends is more fun for everyone involved. Think special and happy instead of spectacular and crabby.

Parents often work too hard and spend too much money on a party that no one enjoys. Life is too short for that. Many families use the *as many friends as your age* rule for a party. If your child is 4-years-old he would invite 4 friends to his party.

What do preschoolers need? They need play and lots of it. They need to play at school and at home. They need to play with friends and on their own. Young children need time to think, play, and explore outdoors.

If you are not all that comfortable outdoors yourself, check out *I Love Dirt* and *Coyote's Guide to Connecting with Nature*. Both books are listed at the end of the chapter under further reading. You will have a great time.

It's difficult to come up with something more developmentally appropriate for preschoolers than time spent outdoors. Children benefit both mentally and physically from being outside in nature. It does wonders for adults too, even if you can only schedule short periods of time for your outdoor adventures.

Any time you spend outside exploring with your child is time well spent, whether you are on a nature trail, in a local park, or in your own backyard the natural world will spur curiosity and build confidence and in your child.

If you are a data minded parent check out the research summaries at the International Journal of Early Childhood Environmental Education at: naturalstart.org/research

Always keep in mind; your preschooler needs quiet time when you can just hang out together inside or outside. **For your child, the gift of your time is better than any toy.**

Some places to find nature programs…

In the D.C./Maryland area much beloved Nature Educator, Amy Beam runs *Kids Love Nature*; a program that brings children and their families into the great outdoors. facebook.com/Kids-Love-Nature-123340972622

In West St. Paul, MN, Dodge Nature Center provides wonderful child and family programs throughout the year. dodgenaturecenter.org

Live on the west coast? You're in luck, so many wonderful nature schools and programs like, The Berkeley Forest School. Berkeleyforestschool.org

There are wonderful programs across the nation.

Find out more about Nature Play and Eco schools from the National Wildlife Association at: nwf.org/Educational-Resources

Wildrock outdoor playscape, Crozet, VA

Further Reading for Parents

Healy, Jane M. *Your Child's Growing Mind: A Practical Guide to Brain Development and Learning from Birth to Adolescence.* (Broadway Books, 2004).

Louv, Richard. *Last Child in the Woods.* (Algonquin Books, 2008).

Siegel, Daniel J. and Bryson, Tina Payne. *The Whole Brain Child: 12 Revolutionary Strategies to Nurture Your Child's Developing Mind.* (Delacorte Press, Random House Publishing Group, 2011).

Ward, Jennifer. *I Love Dirt.* (Trumpeter Books, an imprint of Shambhala Publications, Inc., 2008).

Young, Jon; McGown, Evan; Haas, Ellen. *Coyote's Guide to Connecting with Nature.* (Owlink Media, 2010).

Books to Share with Your Child

Boston, Marc. *The Girl Who Carried Too Much Stuff.* (Juju Seeds Media, LLC. 2015).

Pova, Rosie J. *Sunday Rain.* (Lantana Publishing Ltd. 2021)

6

THE PARENT-TEACHER PARTNERSHIP

Key Factors:

A good teacher will strive to involve and communicate with parents at the preschool.

If you have concerns or questions, you need to inform your child's teacher.

The teacher's priority should be the children's safety and comfort level.

Learning to play with others and growing independence are the two most important outcomes for children who attend preschool.

Conferences are one of the fundamental ways parents and teachers get together and address issues.

If you are looking for specific information regarding your child, let the teacher know before the meeting so there will be no surprises.

How can you work through a Parent – Teacher conflict? Quick resolution is best for everyone.

If you have a negative interaction with your child's teacher, you can try to re-set the relationship.

It can be hard for a teacher to handle every situation in a nuanced way with so many children and parents at a school.

∽

What is the role of the preschool teacher?

The Preschool teacher is not a replacement or surrogate for a child's parents. A preschool teacher is also not a babysitter. They generally pay babysitters much more, if you charge by the hour. I mention this not as a complaint, but just a fact you should know. People choose a teaching career because they love children and families, not because they will get a big paycheck.

A professional teacher has a special role in the development of a child–that of bringing the child into a larger world while respecting both the child, and the parents' sensibilities.

It can be difficult for a teacher to meet the needs of all the parents. Especially since some may be sending their child out into the world, away from family, for the first time. This can be the case at the start of the school year. Teachers are trying to learn all about their new students, so be patient. Let the teacher know if you have concerns or need to meet, but be aware it takes time for everyone to get used to a new schedule.

A good teacher will strive to involve and communicate with parents at the preschool. Communication is a two-way street. Parents need to keep the teacher informed of any important developments, including anything unusual or specific to your child.

A good example would be a child with sensory sensitivity. Let the teacher know in advance that your child has difficulty with unfamiliar sounds, or touching sand. It will help the teacher create a calmer day for your child. If your child is suddenly upset, this information will help the teacher find a solution to the situation much more efficiently.

If you have concerns or questions, you need to inform your child's teacher. Beginning preschool can be even more emotional and difficult for some parents than it is for their child. Make your concerns known to the teacher. The teacher will be focused on your child, and may not realize you are worried.

Parents who out of politeness, shyness, or uncertainty, don't discuss their concerns with the teacher, may end up unhappy with their preschool experience even if the school is a good fit for their child. You need to feel comfortable and understood in the preschool setting. Your child's teacher does not know what you are thinking unless you speak up.

A parent whose child attended a preschool over a decade ago did not understand an aspect of the preschool and joked about "not passing preschool." If only that parent had said something at the time! I know both of the teachers at the school, and they did not know there was any problem. The teachers assumed both parent and child were doing great, because from the teachers' perspective they were.

The teacher's priority should be the children's safety and comfort level. After safety and comfort, the teacher's next priority is each child's growth in social skills, cognitive skills, and physical development. Now add to that the needs, questions, and concerns of all the parents and it has to be a partnership.

At its best, the partnership has parents and teachers respectfully working together in the child's interest. And to support one another. We will talk more about this partnership later in the chapter. For now, let's concentrate on some of what your child's teacher is trying to facilitate at school.

Early in the school year, preschool teachers do their best to get to know each student. As a teacher, I want to help the children take ownership of the school. I want each child to feel comfortable asking for help if needed.

A large part of a teacher's job is to monitor each child's development. At the beginning of the year teachers watch and listen to children to get an idea of where the new class stands with motor skills, cognitive skills, and the ever-important social skills. Teachers achieve this through play, by watching peer interaction, and by watching a child's interaction with adults.

Teachers try to learn about each child's likes, interests, and dislikes. We notice where each child is when using things like scissors and glue bottles. Can her peers understand her? Can she go down the slide on her own? Is she able to share toys? As teachers get to know where each child is developmentally, classrooms and plans can be changed so the "play" at school will meet the new students' needs and expand their experiences.

Learning to play with others and growing independence are the two most important outcomes for children who attend preschool. Teachers, like parents, try to find that balance between watching and guiding children. We may need to help by sharing words children can use like, "Can I play with you?" and stepping in when necessary.

We try to keep our ears and eyes open to know when a child is ready for the next step in play or projects. Often, we just make sure materials for the next step are available when the child is ready, so we don't push the child. We watch to see how we can use one child's excitement in learning to build a tower or putting together a puzzle, to bring in other children so everyone can learn together.

Now let's focus on assessments and preschoolers.

Over the years, I have been part of several federally funded preschool student assessment projects. Including, programs designed by Curry School of Education at the University of Virginia and the University of Chicago.

They tasked these studies with creating classroom assessments for preschools. This is a difficult proposition. Everyone wants an easy checklist, but that is just not possible or appropriate for preschoolers. Children develop at different rates and the more you know about how the brain develops at this age, the more you know this type of assessment can cause more problems than it solves.

Teachers need to track child progress and development. Reggio schools do an outstanding job of documenting a child's growth progress through pictures and stories to share with parents. Just watch out for schools that spend more time assessing children than teaching them and allowing them to play.

What your child's teacher can give you is information regarding her progress at school. A teacher should also be able to tell you if there are any areas in particular that are focused on during your child's school day.

For example, your child's teacher may notice a lack of motor skill confidence and regularly takes the time to encourage and assist your child to go down the slide or kick a ball. Perhaps your child is easily frustrated and hits other children when she wants to use a toy. After talking with her, the teacher may help her practice asking for the toy. Depending on her needs, the teacher will come up with specific options to help your child wait for a turn. In a case like this, I expect the teacher would be in touch with you to form a consistent plan that can be used both at home and at school.

It's best for the child if the parents and teachers work as a team and communicate regularly. Consistency is important for modifying behaviors. Conferences can aid in making sure the adults in a child's life take time to learn from each other and coordinate efforts.

Moira had a hard time speaking when asked a question, especially if people were watching. After a while, children stopped waiting for an answer and would walk away. Moira had a couple of other speech issues. It was hard for her friends to understand her. Her teachers requested a conference with her parents.

Her parents decided she might need to be seen by a specialist. The specialist helped with the speech issues. In a matter of weeks, Moira could communicate in a much more fulfilling way with her friends. Still, she had a hard time answering those questions. The specialist suggested that Moira just say, "Wait a minute, I'm thinking." That would give her time to form an answer, and the other children would not think she was ignoring them.

Moira practiced at home with her parents, and her teachers reminded her to use those words at school. It worked like a charm. Here, it was the parents, teachers, and specialist working together that helped solve the problem. It was great for Moira, because all the adults in her life were consistent in handling her speech issues.

Parents and teachers working together make the most progress for children as they face various issues at school. **Conferences are one of the fundamental ways parents and teachers get together and address issues.**

If you talk to ten parents about conferences, you will get ten different ideas of what a preschool conference should include. Teachers can receive requests from some parents for more assessments on all kinds of developmental issues. Other parents feel any assessments are inappropriate for preschoolers. So how can conferences work for teachers and parents?

It's all about expectations and balance. Both parents and teachers need to enter a conference realizing that everyone wants what's best for the child. We are on the same team.

Teachers and parents need to share important information with each other because they come from different perspectives. Many children behave differently at home than at school. This information helps both the teacher and the parents learn more about the child. Parent-teacher conferences can provide a better understanding for the adults who are most influential in the child's life.

If you are looking for specific information regarding your child, let the teacher know before the meeting so there will be no surprises. If, for example, you worry that your child is rough with other children, making the teacher aware of your concern allows him to take the time to observe your child's actions at school regarding specific behaviors. He will also have time to focus on workable solutions. Your expectations are much more likely to be met and the conference will be much more productive.

You are the expert on your child, and your child's teacher may ask some questions of you to get a fuller understanding of your child. Some questions may be a simple as, *what does your child say about school at home?*

You should have time to ask your questions regarding your child's behavior and growth at school. The teacher is used to working with many children of this age, and guided by that experience, he can tell you if any of your child's development is outside of the normal range.

Let's say the teacher has a concern. It's hard to hear this kind of advice and not take it negatively. Be sure you are listening to what the teacher is saying and not taking his observations as an attack. As a parent, it's easy to view observations and questions from a teacher emotionally. We often take suggestions about our children as criticism.

A professional teacher is thinking about what activities or practices will be the most helpful in your child's development and may not realize that you are viewing the observation as a criticism. Be sure to let your teacher know your feelings.

It may be possible that the "ability" being discussed is one you don't want the teacher to address. This happened with my son in kindergarten. His teacher was concerned about his ability in a reading group. He was doing everything one would expect for pre-reading at home, although a few months behind what our first child did. He was on track in his own time. From my perspective, there were no concerns about his reading ability.

I worried that they might pull him out of his normal class. So, I shared my concerns with a fellow teacher; she felt the kindergarten teacher had a checklist. It turned out the administration had given the teacher a checklist to be filled out for each child. The teacher wasn't worried about my son either. I asked her to mark that the parent was informed and does not want any further action taken at this point. Within a couple years my son was testing out of elementary school reading levels and is an avid reader to this day.

Hopefully you won't have to deal with the early pushing of inappropriate academics at your child's preschool, but if you do, clear communication will keep the parent - teacher relationship in great shape and make it beneficial for your child, which is the ultimate goal. I was fortunate to get advice from a trusted educator to resolve the situation. Make sure your advisors know their field.

I recently read a book by two young academic authors in the field of parenting. It was useful, but in some ways not practical and not a very realistic view of many of the preschools and preschoolers I've worked with over the past few decades.

As I read more about the authors, I learned they wrote this book as part of their doctoral degrees, while they were raising their own young children, the oldest of which was a 3-year-old. That is quite an impressive feat. That fact explained some issues I had with the book. It's hard to possess a full understanding of a subject when you are in the middle of it yourself. The book had a good deal of useful information. The authors were just missing some parts of the puzzle and a little experience.

That is why it's so important that you make use of the parent–teacher relationship. You get the teacher's experience and the teacher gets your expertise regarding your unique child and family dynamic.

How can you work through a Parent-Teacher conflict? Quick resolution is best for everyone.

A smooth school year is all about expectations and communication. If a genuine conflict arises with a teacher or school, schedule a conference when you are not rushed and both sides can voice concerns and listen. Meet as soon as possible. Minor worries can nag at you and grow out of proportion.

Emotions can run strong when dealing with what's best for your child, so it's important to remember you are both on the same team. As a parent, you will put your child's interests above everything else, and you should.

A teacher has a very different perspective and has to keep the well-being of all the children in mind. Often the teacher has encountered a certain behavior many times before and can give suggestions for dealing with the behavior. Maybe the teacher thinks this case is similar to ones he has dealt with in the past, but there may be a reason for your child's behavior that only you know.

Parents and teachers need to share this information. The partnership works best when fears and conflicts are addressed quickly and calmly. Make the teacher aware of any situation that is bothering you so that he can address it and will not continue to bother you until it grows out of proportion.

If you have a negative interaction with your child's teacher, you can try to re-set the relationship.

If appropriate, apologize, but if you did or said what was needed, don't apologize for that! Ask to meet with the teacher and be clear about your concerns. Explain why the situation was upsetting. Then you can figure out how to move forward, together. Always consider what is in the best interest of your child. You're sure to find some common ground there.

What do you do if you and your child's teacher just do not agree on an important issue? If a conference hasn't resolved things, your next step depends on the size of the school and the importance of the issue.

Your school may have a director. Contacting that person is the next step. Meeting with the teacher and a third party can be helpful and enlightening for both parties. Sometimes issues resolve when a meeting includes a child's therapist.

If your issue would require major policy changes at the school, or if you believe there is a real danger to your child, you may need to leave that preschool. Sometimes it just isn't the right fit. Your sanity and your child's welfare come first.

If the problem at school involves a behavioral challenge, like hitting, you need to keep a couple things in mind. Behavioral challenges with your child or with other children take time to solve. Don't expect an issue to be resolved overnight. A meeting with the teacher is a first step toward working together.

Depending on the challenge, a solution may involve a change at home or at school. The solution may well require talking with your child about what is at the root of the behavior. This can be tricky with preschoolers, but there are ways to ask about an issue without dwelling on it.

Adults often talk too much about challenges with preschoolers. Sometimes we talk because the child doesn't have the words to express their feelings and as a parent, you may keep talking and trying to guess what is bothering your child. Conferring with her teacher may help you (and the teacher) figure out what the problem is.

The school needs to be welcoming and safe for everyone. A good teacher works to help each child through difficulties and empowers those children by showing them how to handle difficult situations themselves. In preschool, we try to teach children how to handle social situations, giving them tools and words to help them grow in their independence and confidence.

Teachers try to do this in as safe a setting as possible, remembering it's okay to feel bad sometimes. In fact, it's important for a child to learn how to handle anger or sadness before she heads off to kindergarten.

We live at a time when parents are expected to jump in immediately if a child is upset. Children need to be allowed to work through their feelings. Your child may be happy, sad, angry, worried, satisfied, excited, or afraid. These are important feelings, and it takes time to learn how to deal with powerful emotions. For a child, it's empowering to know you can handle emotions yourself.

If your child is having a conflict with another child at school, and emotions are running high, make sure the teacher is aware of your child's situation so he can monitor it and help the children resolve the issue.

When to share private information.

This can be a little tricky in preschool. Perhaps I should say *not* sharing can be tricky. It's part of a teacher's job to keep information confidential. Hopefully you trust your child's teacher. Even in a cooperative school setting, where everyone knows a lot about everyone else's family, if you want something to be confidential just be sure to be clear with the teacher or school administrator.

The problem is preschoolers are just learning social rules. Getting adults to cooperate is one thing, but if your child is going through something unusual at home like parents separating, a seriously ill family member, or a death in the family, it may come up at school.

Make sure the teacher is aware of a serious event so he can field questions and concerns. It's important that your family's views and beliefs regarding the issue are known. That way, the teacher can keep things consistent for your child.

On a funny note, I can't tell you how many little ones have announced at morning meeting that Mom was going to have a baby, long before Mom was ready to announce it! On the serious side, children often need help to process their feelings. The best thing for a child when there has been a major family change, such as a birth or a death in the family, is to keep their routine as regular as possible.

One of my young music students had been alone with her grandfather when he died. After a couple of weeks, her father brought her to music class. I was unaware of the circumstances that had led to her absence from the last couple of classes. At the end of the lesson, she was having a great time dancing with me and I looked over and saw her father crying.

When I got the chance, I asked if everything was alright. He said the music class was the first time since her grandfather died that she had physically let go of her mother or father. Routines and familiar faces help when life's problems crop up.

Sometimes parents and teachers have to work together to resolve unproductive or harmful patterns in a child's behavior. Is your child using upsetting behavior to manipulate the situation in a way that is not good for her in the long run? She may not be consciously doing this. She may just know that a certain negative behavior, like a tantrum, got her what she wanted in another context.

A teacher will not accept that behavior, particularly if it is dangerous to the child or other children at school. Teachers are trained in finding positive ways to help her find an alternate behavior. Parents are often surprised at how quickly a child can independently recover at school, knowing that at home it would have been a long, drawn-out affair.

Expectations are different at school, and one goal is to help your child care for herself. The road to competent adulthood starts here.

Even in a cooperative preschool where parents play a large role, the school is ultimately not set up for you as much as it is set up for your child. That sounds obvious, but it is easy to project your feelings and fears on the situation and not see the big picture regarding the growth of your child. Your child's is learning to handle situations on her own. That's a big deal for her and for you.

Your child will have to work through some problems without your help. That is how self-confidence is built. It's difficult to stand back and let your young child try to handle the situation, whether it is physical (recuperating from a fall) or emotional (Sarah won't let me play with her). See how far your child can go on her own before assuming she needs help.

When a difficult situation pops up, don't assume your child, a teacher, or another parent sees the situation the same way you do. Clear communication is so important. The teacher may not know how you or your child are feeling. Another parent may not know all elements of a situation that bothers you. A teacher may know specifics about a classroom situation.

Remember teachers are human too.

It can be hard for a teacher to handle every situation in a nuanced way with so many children and parents at a school.

One day, I misread a parent who was acting as an assistant teacher in the school. At our school, children may move between three different rooms. A child pulled me out of another room and brought me to the dress-up area to help her. I wondered why she didn't ask the parent who was in the room. I noticed the parent had what seemed like an unhappy look on her face.

The parent was new in town and missed her old home and childcare situation. There was a boisterous group of children having fun playing, building with blocks, and calling out loudly in the room. After helping the little girl put on her new construction worker outfit, I moved a few of the other children out of the room, thinking the parent needed a quieter space.

Later, at a conference, she mentioned this event and how the kids should be able to play and not be kiboshed. She was right, and I should have asked her if she was okay with the excitement in the room. Nobody is perfect and sometimes a teacher can make a bad call, even with the best of intentions. I misread her, and that caused her to misread how I handled the children and the play in that room.

The bottom line is positive communication. Contact the teacher as soon as possible if you have concerns or questions about a situation. The only caveat is do not bring up an important subject with a teacher right before school is about to start in the morning. Unless it is something the teacher needs to know for that day. It's fine to ask when you can call or meet, but as the school day is about to begin, you want that teacher focused on the children and the day ahead.

Further Reading for Parents

Christakis, Erika. *The Importance of Being Little: What Preschoolers Really Need from Grownups.* (Viking, 2016).

Parents.com 20 Tips for Parents from Preschool Teachers

7

WORRIES AND FEARS

Key Factors:

It's important not to let worry stop you and your child from enjoying life.

Separating from parents is a big step.

It is important that the adults in a child's life communicate with and support each other.

Are you the one who is struggling with separation anxiety?

Know in advance how the school handles an upset child.

Many parents find it helpful to have a plan of action on a day when separation is difficult.

Good life skills start young while you, the parent, are there to make sure choices are safe and appropriate.

For parents and teachers, mistakes are golden opportunities.

A big cause of worries and poor decision-making is lack of sleep.

Really listen to what the child is saying. What is the actual fear?

Listening is your most important tool. It honors and respects the child.

Parents of 3- to 5-year-olds get concerned when their child lies.

Sometimes worry, justified or not, gets the best of us. **It's important not to let worry stop you and your child from enjoying life**, learning, and growing together. For some families, worrying becomes a real burden for parents and children alike. Too much worrying can cause you to miss out on all the good things that are happening each day.

In this chapter, we will discuss some fears that commonly manifest themselves during the preschool years. We will look at everything from monsters under the bed to the death of a loved one. Let's start with one of the most pervasive and frustrating worries, separation anxiety.

Separation Anxiety

Some form of separation anxiety is almost universal. It can happen when a child is very young, or at preschool, and even in elementary school. For some children it is not a big issue; for others it can be cyclical and continue to return long after you thought it was over.

Separating from parents is a big step. It can be difficult, but it's so important for your child to know you believe in him. That will allow him to believe in himself. This is the beginning of creating an independent, self-confident adult. You, your child, and your child's teacher must build a relationship of trust. My parent is gone, but my teacher is here if I need help.

It's hard for any parent to see their child upset without wanting to make the situation better right away. Separation anxiety may be a tough one for you, if you tend to jump in before giving your child a chance to work things out on his own. This type of anxiety only goes away if you set the example for your child. Sometimes you have to be strong for your child's benefit, and yours.

If you are insecure about leaving your child at school, your child will also be insecure about school and may not even understand why. Do your homework and leave your child in competent and kind hands. If your child expresses concerns, explain to him that those feelings are normal and don't dwell on it. Acknowledge the feelings and move on to another topic.

Talk to your child's teacher about strategies for handling separation anxiety. Together, you can make a plan. Learn the school's morning routine so you can answer any questions your child might have. And you can be confident that you know what is happening while your child is at school.

Like many new challenges, this is a great opportunity. Help your child to grow and trust that he can handle things on his own and be his own person (in a safe environment). This is an early step toward independence.

There are preschoolers who can separate with ease and college students who still can't quite let go. Learning to separate is part personality and part practice. If you find the right tools to help your child, your mornings will be happier and calmer. Your child will gain greater personal power and self-confidence.

School drop-off is different from leaving your child with a friend or family member. This is how he becomes part of a group beyond family. Remember, the teacher is dealing with all the children. A solution that may work for your child at home may not work at school. If a solution for your child causes three other children to cry, then that's not the right solution for the group.

Let's say the school doesn't allow children to bring their own food or drink. Maia's dad doesn't want Maia to cry when he leaves. At home she has a special sippy cup that soothes her. Dad wants to bring in Maia's cup so she won't cry when he leaves the school. Now the teacher has to deal with several children who all want Maia's cup or want to bring in a cup from home. One child may even try to take Maia's special cup. School differs from home, but don't worry. Together Maia's dad and the teacher will find the right solution. This is what preschool teachers do.

Here are examples of two very different scenarios of children with separation anxiety:

Justin, an only child, was attending his first day of preschool. It was also his first day of any regularly scheduled activity on his own. Naturally, he was apprehensive about his parents leaving.

In this case, his mother was sure he was going to cry, and that she was going to cry too. She spoke with the teacher in advance. Together, they told Justin that Mom would leave before morning circle. Mom had to follow through, even though it was going to be hard. The children were called to the circle. Mom handed Justin to the teacher, who took him to check out the fish tank as Mom went out the door.

In less than five minutes, Justin was sitting with the teacher at morning circle learning the names of his new friends, and a teaching assistant was running out the door to tell Justin's Mom all was well. By the second week, there were no tears. Justin had adjusted to the schedule. He tried crying a couple more mornings in the first week, but it changed nothing so he stopped that behavior at school. Is this typical? Yes. But it is not a one size fits all approach.

An older child, Aisha, was very used to school and had no problem separating. She would skip off to play with her friends when she arrived at school in the mornings. Over the summer, her mother had surgery. Mom was in the hospital for a while and could not do much for a couple of weeks when she returned home.

When school started in the fall, Aisha was in a panic. She wanted to go to school, but did not want to leave her mother's side. It was understandable that she feared something could happen to her mother. In response to Aisha's fears, her mother came to school with her. It was acceptable, since this school allowed parents to join in whenever they wanted. After some time had passed, this routine was putting stress on the family and the parents asked for advice to help Aisha get back to being independent.

Aisha's teacher asked the parents to make sure Aisha knew Mom was fine now, and that they were not hiding anything from her.

Next, they set up a schedule with Aisha. Her parents explained that Mom needed time to do her work, and if she worked while Aisha was at school, then they could spend time together after school. Together with Aisha, they looked at the calendar and picked a day in the next week when Aisha would come to school with Dad. They agreed Dad would leave before morning meeting. They marked the day on the family calendar. On that day, Dad brought Aisha to school in the morning and watched her run off with friends right away. No tears and no turning back.

In this example, a calm solution took some time to implement. That was an appropriate resolution, since the situation had gone on for some time. Aisha's summer experience had been scary and difficult for her. She was quite a mature preschooler and needed to be treated as such. It was important that she had a role in the solution.

Aisha's parents made sure each step was clear. Then they followed through by doing everything exactly as they said they would. I have used this approach many times. Involve the child in the solution and be clear that a change is needed.

The best solutions are calm, honest, and consistent. The child is often involved in making the plan. **It is important that the adults in a child's life communicate with and support each other.**

Here is something to consider. **Are you the one who is struggling with separation anxiety?** Your feelings are as real and important as your child's. The advice for you is the same as the earlier advice for helping your child through this; acknowledge your feelings, but don't dwell on them.

Your feelings are instinctual. We are programed as parents to protect our little ones. When you are leaving a distraught child with others, your lower brain kicks in and wants you to protect your child. If you are struggling at separation time, you need two things. You need to be confident you are leaving your child in a safe place with capable, compassionate people, and you need to have practiced how you will leave ahead of time in your mind.

More than one parent has confided in me that after leaving their child, they just went to the car, sat down and cried. It happens and maybe you need a minute to do that, but here are some other ideas.

Know in advance how the school handles an upset child. Teachers are well versed in this, and although it is different for each child, there are some common actions.

In most preschools, if a child is crying and upset, the teacher will hold the child, except for those children who prefer not to be held. Teachers have a lot of practice at comforting children. Many schools set a time limit and will call you if the child is crying and can't seem to settle down. It is rare to have a child continue to be upset for long, after the parent leaves. The tears are real, but they are for your benefit. Once the parent has left, most children look for something fun to do or someone to play with. As a parent, it's nice to know how you will be contacted if your child needs you.

As a teacher, I will tell you I have occasionally called a parent if I could get away, to tell them their child was settled in and playing. When you leave a crying child, that image stays in your mind even if your child started to play a few minutes after you left. Children often move through emotions faster than adults.

Some parents are concerned about the teacher. After all, their child is not the only child in the school. They worry that the teacher will have to focus on just their child. So here is a reminder. This is what teachers are trained to do. Helping children learn how best to comfort themselves and gain a sense of control is a big deal and an important lesson.

As much as I care for your child, as a teacher, those tears affect me, but not in the same primal way they affect you. I see the tears as an opportunity to grow and learn. Every time he maneuvers through these emotions, your child will get stronger and gain more control. A good preschool is a safe setting for this important growth to take place.

In the same way that it is helpful for your child to know how the day is going to go, **many parents find it helpful to have a plan of action on a day when separation is difficult.**

You could plan to tackle an engaging project at work. You could meet with a friend for coffee or tea. It's hard to ease your mind if you are used to being home with your child and now your child is not there. No matter how many times you think to yourself, *I can't wait for school to start, then I can do all these things I've been wanting to get to.* It can still be hard the first few days to start the new routine.

It can be difficult to focus if you just left a crying child. One of the best things you can do is exercise if your schedule allows it. If you come from a family that exercises routinely, then you are already aware of the benefits. Try a 20-minute walk out in the fresh air. That can change your perspective for the better. Have a plan to do something or meet with someone, after you drop off your child.

The most important tip I can give you after years of watching how families handle separation anxiety and seeing over and over what works and what does not work, is to tell the truth. Never sneak out on your child because you can't bear to see him cry. This will prolong the problem and cause greater anxiety in your child, along with more crying and clinginess. It may be easier for you that day, but it will make him fearful and his world will seem unpredictable. Your child will wonder if you are going to disappear every time he turns away. Don't put that unnecessary stress in your child's life.

Tell your child when you are going to leave and then follow through. Surprises are the enemy when building a drop-off routine. We want to build trust. It may be hard for you, but keep in mind you are doing this for your child.

If you tell your child you will leave at a certain time, perhaps before morning meeting, and then let him talk you into staying for meeting, guess what happens. Now your child realizes, as those intelligent little ones always do, that he can change your mind. Your job has just become much harder. Your morning routine (and your child's) will now be much more stressful.

Children and adults are stressed when they're not sure what to expect. By changing your mind, you have created a situation where neither you nor your child know what to expect the next few mornings. That's why many schools handle this for you. They do not allow parents to stay so there is no choice. You may want that in a school, if you don't have the strength to handle separation yourself.

If there is no choice, you have to go and your child knows that. Another solution is a preschool that helps the child and parent make this transition together and not by force. The world is full of options.

It is amazing how a child will stop crying when their parent leaves. I have seen children sit right down to meeting talking and playing as if nothing happened while their parent is a few yards away in tears. When you see your child acting like the world is ending, it's hard to imagine that they are not still upset after you've leave.

I have zipped out the door to tell a parent who hasn't even made it out of the building yet, that their child is already laughing with a friend. Does that happen every time? Absolutely not. Your child's teacher needs to have the same respect for you that I ask you to have for your child. This means telling you the truth about how your child is doing. Sometimes a child takes a while to recover and a teacher will help your child (and you) find the best tools to make that big step.

One of the worst things about separation anxiety is that it is often cyclical. Parents may return to school a second year thinking separation anxiety will not be a problem. Unfortunately, for some families, the worry is back. It's best to minimize reaction and remind your child *we've been through this before.*

If your child has a specific complaint, be sure to take it seriously. It may be something you want to share with the teacher. Be careful not to over react. I have seen young children figure out what concerns their parents the most and use that knowledge to control a parent. A child who has figured out this type of scenario will bring up their parent's fears.

Here's a perfect example of the importance of getting the entire story and not jumping to conclusions. On the first day of school one year, Danny hit his new friend Keenan. He wasn't even sure why he did it. Danny and Keenan were both crying. After that day, Danny and Keenan became good friends, but Keenan remembered this incident upset his father. As can often happen, it seemed to bother the parent more than the child. Three weeks later, Keenan did not want his father to leave one morning.

> Keenan told his father, "I'm afraid."
>
> His Dad asked, "What's wrong?"
>
> Keenan replied, "I'm afraid Danny will hit me."
>
> His father started to get upset until the teacher asked, "When has Danny hit you?"
>
> Keenan said, "The first day of school."
>
> The teacher calmly responded, "Oh, remember we talked about that and Danny said he was sorry. Has he ever hit you again?"
>
> Keenan replied, "No."
>
> This was the perfect opportunity for the teacher to say, "I think Danny is waiting for you with John at the blocks."

Keenan ran off to join his friends, and Dad could leave. Those two families ended up forming a friendship that has lasted years.

Separation anxiety may be part of your child's make-up. You may need to help him understand his own feelings. Many times, a child who can't wait to start school has no problem in the beginning, but when the novelty of school has worn off, he cries and grabs onto the parent at drop off time. While it is important to ask your child if something has prompted this change, it may just be time for checking the limits and regularity of the morning routine.

Clear communication is important. Once something is said, don't over talk it. When a parent is struggling with separation, experienced teachers can tell if the parent will make it out the door by whether they allow themselves to be drawn into a long explanation of things the child already knows.

Children know that if they can just get their parent to talk– well, they may very well get their way. Who wouldn't want to have a person who loves them at their beck and call? Unless there is something unusual going on that day, be strong. The consistency of a normal routine will comfort your child.

Children and adults do best when expectations are met. Although it may seem like you are meeting their needs by changing your mind about leaving or staying, it just causes a lot of unnecessary confusion and stress for your child.

Keep your eye on the prize. The actual goal is helping your child to become an independent, competent person. Preschool is where it starts. Children need to believe they are competent in their world and can handle going to school.

A preschooler can pick out his own clothes, brush his hair, go to preschool, and more. Parents and teachers have to allow children to trust in their own competence. Coddled children and adults lack confidence and always seek the guidance from others, which can lead them astray when you're not around. **Good life skills start young while you, the parent, are there to make sure choices are safe and appropriate.**

How does the school handle problems that pop up?

Some parents worry about leaving their child at preschool because they are unsure how he will be treated if he does something "wrong." If you feel this way, be sure to ask the school director or preschool teacher how issues at school are handled. For minor issues, teachers often just redirect children to another activity.

Your child needs two things; an understanding of expectations and a feeling of security. Teachers create a safe learning environment by focusing on concrete behavior examples for the child.

Abstract rules mean little to a young child. In working out rules of behavior it is so important to remember, children do not think like adults, with abstract requests. "Be fair" and "Be kind to others" are important concepts to introduce and explain to preschoolers. In the heat of the moment, many children take those phrases to mean that the adult or other child should give them what they want or let them do what they want because that would be "being kind to them." Young children need to understand expectations, and those expectations need to be consistent.

For Joelle, ramming her tricycle into Tricia's tricycle may seem like fun. She is not trying to be unkind. Joelle may be trying to play with Tricia and may not understand why Tricia is upset. I like to explain why the behavior is dangerous and clarify that at school we may not ram our tricycle into another tricycle.

Joelle needs to know the rule, the reason for the rule, and what will happen if she does it again. Then, I ask Joelle if she understands the rule. Does she understand what will happen, if she runs into another tricycle again? Joelle now knows that if she runs into a tricycle, she will have to get off her tricycle. She will get to try riding again the next day, but she's done riding for today.

I want Joelle to be aware of the school rules and what will happen if she breaks the rules, in very clear concrete terms. Anything else is both unfair and unsafe for Joelle and all the other children at the school.

For some children, a school rule like this is one of the first times they experience an adult who is clear and then calmly enforces the consequence. When safety is involved and everyone is clear on the rules, there is no *one more chance*. Well, there is another chance, and that chance will be tomorrow. So, let's find something else to play today.

Great learning comes from conflict. These moments are opportunities to grow, to understand someone else's feelings, to learn that you have to be careful when your actions affect others. Honestly, conflict is what preschool is about. If your child already knows how to handle every social situation, then he does not need preschool.

Conflict is great - it's why we are all here. When a conflict occurs, be sure to ask the children involved to tell you what happened. It may vary from what you think happened. You may only have seen one child's behavior when another child may have initiated the encounter. If it is a matter of sharing, we often ask the children if they have ideas for a solution and if their idea works for everyone, we make sure they follow through with that resolution.

For Adults: Mistakes = Opportunities

Some parents worry they will make mistakes. Yes, you will make mistakes. We all do. **For parents and teachers,**

mistakes are golden opportunities. We all learn the most from our mistakes.

Be genuine when you realize you made a mistake. You should do your best to correct the situation if possible. This is an opportunity for your child to see you as an individual, just like him. There are parents who worry that admitting they were wrong will undermine their child's respect. In my experience, that is not the case.

Children learn by example. You might say, "I'm sorry. I was wrong." When you apologize and do your best to correct the situation, your child learns what to do when he makes mistakes. It's okay to acknowledge it's hard to say "Sorry," when you have done something wrong, but it's the best thing to do. Then everyone involved can move on.

Parents may worry that they've overreacted. Sometimes an adult will speak in haste because a child's action did not meet their expectations. "Why didn't you go with your Father? It's Father's Day!" This can cause undue guilt or shame for a child. At times all you can do is make a mental note to be more careful in the future.

I'm not condoning inappropriate behavior. We all want our children to understand that their actions have consequences, but we don't want to put unnecessary stress on a child who has done or said something with no malice intended. We cannot expect a young child to have the same perspective as an adult.

Don't put undue pressure on your preschooler. It is very stressful for 3- and 4-year-olds to make important decisions and it's just not appropriate. As much as we want to encourage independent thinking and decision making, sometimes you need to be the adult to provide a safe, calm atmosphere.

Children find security in knowing someone is in charge. Someone is looking out for them. It is just not fair to the child to expect them to set their own bedtimes, to decide if they are going to school, or make any big decision that has larger implications for their health and well-being.

One parent expressed concern for her son. He would only eat two foods, one of which was a cookie. Since the parent was the person who buys and prepares the food, we came up with a list of foods to buy. The list included fruit, vegetables, and other reasonable snacks to have on hand.

The parent set out three food choices at snack time and left the decision of what to eat up to her son. It worked. If it had not worked, we would have come up with another plan. But hungry children will usually eat if given a choice of a few foods. This families' actual story sounds simplistic, but it's very common for parents to become overwhelmed and it's easy to fall back on unhealthy habits.

It can help to get another person's perspective on a situation. Talk to someone who is not invested in the battle of wills. Someone who has a little distance and experience can often provide simple suggestions that are hard to see when you're at an impasse.

We have covered several common worries and fears of children and parents. Worries get blown out of proportion when parents don't get enough sleep. This can be a universal problem when you have small children in the house.

A big cause of worries and poor decision-making is lack of sleep. I speak as a parent whose second child was a very light sleeper for the first 2 years. I had no idea how fuzzy my brain was until he started sleeping through the night. That's when I started sleeping again. It's hard not to worry about things if you're not sleeping. Tips for child/family evening routines are in Chapter 2. Never underestimate how important it is to get a good night's sleep when it comes to everyone's health, energy, and peace of mind.

Preschooler's Worries

There can be a lot to worry about in life, even for little people. Around the age of four, preschoolers think about a lot of issues; from monsters under the bed to why did grandpa die. Sometimes we cause fears. That's okay, because life lessons need to be practiced. It's about how you handle the situation. You can try to be careful not to create fears where there are none. Just because you feared something doesn't mean your child will.

Be sure to listen to what your child is saying and be careful not to introduce fears that are not there. One parent described how a relative sent them a book about monsters under the bed. The parent read the book to her son, who had never thought of such a thing as monsters under the bed. I'm sure you have already figured out that her little boy developed a big fear of monsters under his bed.

Fortunately, the fear was handled with the old spray bottle filled with water and marked *MONSTER BE GONE*. After a bedtime story each night, Mom would mist under the bed and anywhere else a monster could hide. Adding a little lavender to the spray bottle can be a nice relaxing touch.

It's easy to cause new fears. The best thing we all can do is **really listen to what the child is saying. What is the actual**

fear? Be vigilant, especially where there is a big change in a child's life such as a move, a death in the family, divorce, or a change in schools.

Ask your child questions about what they understand so you can comfort them. Be honest and factual but *don't answer more than is asked*. Most adults talk too much and try to give more information than a young child wants or can understand. Over talking can cause new fears.

Children at this age may ask about death, especially if a relative or family friend passes away. A child may internalize that fear. *Will my parent die? Will I die soon?* I recommend you don't approach your child with the idea of death, but if they verbalize the fear, comfort them and let them know they are fine and Aunt Liza had been ill for some time. We were expecting her passing or whatever is the appropriate and simplest truth you can convey.

Don't avoid a difficult topic; just don't dwell on it even if your child wishes to. Children rarely are as stressed out about a death as a parent is. Try not to reflect your feelings in their questions. Listen to what your child is asking and answer succinctly.

If there is a major change in a child's life, adults in the child's life need to communicate calmly and consistently. You should inform anyone who regularly spends time with your child of the change and how you are handling it.

Parents can be concerned when a child does not seem to care that an older relative has died. Do not assume that your child does not care about others. Many preschoolers don't understand how final death is.

It may also be the case that they don't know the older relative that well. You, the parents, are your child's core family.

For children, as long as you're okay, they're okay. Your grandfather's death may have been a tough time for you, but if your child spent little time with him, your child may not show any feelings regarding the death. Do your best to keep your child's routines normal while making some time to care for yourself.

One family I work with was separating. The parents did a wonderful job of seeing each other as a family and both helping with parenting the child. One day Zoe was so fretful that I sat down with her and asked what was wrong. It turns out that in all the explaining everyone had done regarding the new home situation, no one had ever told her where the family pet was going to live and she had it in her mind she would leave her cat behind.

At the end of the school day, Zoe and I sat down with her parents and talked. They had noticed her sadness over the preceding days and assumed it was the separation. I can't tell you how relieved they were when they realized what was bothering her. Zoe was visibly relieved to learn that her cat would stay with her.

The best advice is to keep the worrying to a minimum. Try to enjoy the moment and remind yourself not to worry about the future. You can handle it when it arrives. Make your life into the life you wish for your child. Children copy what they learn from you. If you always feel stressed and worried, your child will start to feel that way, too. Having children is a great opportunity for you to reevaluate who you want to be. People who are always worried are living in the future, not the present.

When worries appear, **listening is your most important tool. It honors and respects the child.** It allows him to know that he has been heard. "I hear you. You want that toy, but someone else is playing with it now." He may not like your response, but he knows your listening. That means a lot to a child. Listening and responding build trust and respect.

Lies

One last worry to mention; lies. **Parents of 3- to 5-year-olds often get concerned when their child lies.** One more fun fact for preschool parents is that this is when children start this important mental development. This is the age when children figure out other people perceive things differently than they do. *I thought the cookie was for me, but I don't think Mom did, so I'll tell her the dog ate it.*

No one seeks to encourage unwanted behavior, but lying really is an important mental development and not a sign of a "bad" child. It's normal and should be corrected calmly. You can tell your child you know the dog didn't eat the cookie. Unless you notice your child becoming a habitual liar, it is usually not a problem, just a growth stage.

Further Reading for Parents

Carter, Christine. *Raising Happiness, 10 Simple Steps for More Joyful Kids and Happier Parents*. (Ballantine Books, 2011).

Eisen, Andrew R., Engler, Linda B., Sparrow, Joshua. *Helping Your Child Overcome Separation Anxiety or School Refusal: A Step-By-Step Guide for Parents*. (New Harbinger Publications, Inc. 2006).

Books to Share with Your Child

Appelt, Kathi. *Oh My Baby, Little One*. (Harcourt Children's Books, 2006).

Cohen, Miriam and Himler, Ronald. *Will I Have a Friend?* (Star Bright Books, 2009).

Northway, Jennifer. *See you later Mum!* (Frances Lincoln Children's Books, 2006).

Penn, Audrey. *The Kissing Hand*. (Tanglewood Press, Inc., 2006).

8
TOILET TRAINING & TANTRUMS

Key Factors:

These phases usually pass very quickly.

Every situation is different and there are legitimate reasons for a variety of techniques and timing.

If you miss the opportune time, you may have a little one in diapers for quite a while.

What are the signs that your child is ready to move out of diapers?

There are many positives to getting out of diapers. Avoiding diaper rash and diaper related bladder infections are high on the list.

Start with a relaxed week at home where you expect accidents and can make it a calmer transition overall.

Children who have full-blown tantrums (which often includes throwing themselves on the floor) are generally feeling rushed, stressed, exhausted, pressured, or a loss of control.

Notice the circumstances when your child has a tantrum.

You will not react well under stress if you do not already have a plan.

Parenting is about knowing yourself as much as it is about knowing your child.

∼

The Fun Chapter!

Now for the topics that get a special little chapter of their own because they can seem overwhelming. **These phases usually pass very quickly,** but to an exhausted parent it can seem like an eternity. Some issues can even return at a later date just when you think you've got them under control.

There are many books and plenty of advice on handling these topics from professionals and experts. Find a philosophy that resonates with you and stick to your plan. In the middle of one of these challenges, everyone from grandpas to strangers tends to weigh in with suggestions.

Keep in mind that **every situation is different and there are legitimate reasons for a variety of techniques and timing.** I have included a brief book list and website list on these topics at the end of the chapter. Check online as well since new ideas and new publications regarding best practices come out every month. Keep in mind that not every book is for every family.

Let's start with learning to use the toilet.

There will always be the individual child or family for whom the case can be made to hold off on using the toilet because of medical, physical, or psychological reasons including stressful family events. There will also always be the case for some to train very young because they are interested and ready. The trick is to make sure what you are doing is in the best interest of your child and not waiting because you don't have the time to set aside to help your child make this big step calmly.

Try to find the time and a plan for when your child is ready. **If you miss the opportune time, you may have a little one in diapers for quite a while.** We want this to be a challenge your child can master and avoid a battle of wills.

For most children, the opportune time is between 18 months and 30 months. Yes, that's an entire year, because no two children are the same. So, **what are the signs that your child is ready to move out of diapers?** Is she curious about the toilet? Maybe she asks about it or wants to watch other people use the toilet. Is her diaper dry for longer than usual, even through naps? That is a sign of some control. Does she know before she is about to urinate or have a bowel movement?

Wet diapers bother many children. That's a great incentive for training. No one wants to be in wet pants. If your child is voicing this discomfort, you can say, "That's why we go in the toilet."

Toilet training can seem like a Sisyphean feat when you are going through it. In reality, it usually takes a short time. Have a plan and stick to it. Be clear about expectations with your child and talk very little about it. Continue on through the process calmly doing what needs to be done; reminders, patience, cleanups, and positive reinforcement.

At school, parents often tell me their child is doing pretty well at home, but they put her in pull-ups for school "just in case." Don't. Are there ever cases where you should use pull-ups at school? Yes. Check in with your child's teacher.

Accidents in preschool can be handled quickly and calmly. No big deal. What we don't want is for your child to regress. If she wears underwear at home, she should wear underwear at school. Leave extra clothes, including underwear at school and your child is on her way to independence.

In America and Europe, the recent trend has been to lengthen the time in diapers out of a fear of traumatizing the child and due to busy lifestyles. These are countries where many families now consider disposable diapers to be the norm. There are some reasons to avoid joining this trend. Some studies show that waiting too long can occasionally cause health problems.

Then there is the true cost of diapers including landfills and the effect on the environment. Fortunately, convenient washable diapers do exist and are great if you are in a situation where you can plan to run a load of diapers once every day or two. I have listed an example of good cloth diapers at the end of the chapter. It's not an all-or-nothing situation. You may use cloth diapers at home and disposable when out, or at night.

There are many positives to getting out of diapers. Avoiding diaper rash and diaper related bladder infections are high on the list. Psychologically mastering your own body is a big deal. It's a significant achievement for your child and a step toward feeling like a capable "big" kid.

There are also some negative effects of late training, including babying your child instead of promoting an independent "I can do it" philosophy. When you push it off until 4 or 5 years of age, you are also setting your child up to be made fun of by other children or feeling embarrassed in some settings. As adults, we all try to keep children from embarrassing their peers. If an accident happens with an older child, teachers do their best to make the moment a teachable one.

Families with young children and complex schedules are busy rushing from music class to gymnastics to soccer with no time to relax and spend a week around the house. But a few days with no pressure to start potty training is best. I am not saying it will only take a week; although that may be true for those who are ready to go. Most children need to be prepared in advance. After that, try to **start with a relaxed week at home where you expect accidents and can make it a calmer transition overall.**

In the end, this is a big step and life becomes easier for everyone. The goal is to keep everything calm and comfortable. A secure little potty seat or little potty is helpful. Avoid a battle of wills. Learning to use the toilet is a time of growth for the child-parent relationship. For a child, there is a genuine pride of accomplishment in mastering the toilet.

One last note for a few parents. I know that for a few people even talking about toileting is uncomfortable. Some parents think a child shouldn't see an adult using the bathroom. My advice is to treat going to the bathroom like any bodily life skill, such as eating, running, sleeping, washing-up, and brushing teeth. Your child will need your help. If you don't want your child to have toileting issues, be sure to treat using the toilet like the natural necessity it is.

Parentingscience.com Potty Training Tips

Potty Training 101 for parents is also found at...Babycenter.com 3 days to potty training

Cloth diapers, Nickisdiapers.com

They carry lots of different types. It's just a good place to start if you are looking for quality, simple to use, cloth diapers.

Now on to Tantrums

Some children start loud, kicking, screaming, out-of-control tantrums at a young age, while others seem to be tantrum free and suddenly throw one at 3 years of age or older. Tantrums can happen for several reasons, but basically you have a young, frustrated, tired child who has to let it all out.

It can be scary and feel out of control for both the child and parent. The older children are, the more they may use tantrums to get their way. You need a plan of action so you don't encourage tantrums.

Some medical conditions can cause tantrums. I will leave discussion of those tantrums to the medical professionals. If you think something unusual is going on, check in with your pediatrician or family doctor. However, for most children it's a normal phase. Let's go over some causes of tantrums and some general advice.

Children who have full-blown tantrums (which often includes throwing themselves on the floor) are generally feeling rushed, stressed, exhausted, pressured, or a loss of control.

I've noticed three principal causes; overstimulation, frustration, and unfulfilled expectations. **Notice the circumstances when your child has a tantrum.** It often happens in situations that adults are used to dealing with. Noisy places, sizeable crowds, and poor lighting can all contribute to overstimulation for young children.

Two-year-olds often get frustrated because they can't communicate their needs or wants fully through speech yet. If your child is looking forward to something special (perhaps something you are not even aware of), but your plans differ from your child's, that surprise can send a little one over the edge.

Tantrums often happen in large warehouse type stores or grocery stores. Sensitive young children, who are tired of shopping, have to deal with poor lighting and over stimulation from sound and sight. Another common place for a tantrum is at a party or with a group of children. This location can hit all the common triggers.

Know the triggers. Then you can prevent or mitigate them. We all have to go shopping, so think about ways to prepare your child. Discuss where you are going, what it will be like, and what you expect to happen. If you notice your child is getting upset because of a change to the plan, that is a great time to smile and say, "Things don't always go as we plan them." Maybe you can even come up with a reason why this is a pleasant change.

When your child has a tantrum, **you will not react well under stress if you do not already have a plan.** My children had different types of tantrums. My daughter had two full-blown tantrums when she was almost 3 years old. I had just read about tantrums and what you should do. Her tantrums were of the textbook variety, and in this case the textbook solutions worked.

The first tantrum happened while shopping at a department store. Typical for tantrums, we were both tired. I was trying to run some weekly errands and my cart was full. On our way to check out my daughter cried and threw a fit because she wanted some item. I paused and thought, *this is it, and you know what to do.* As a person who grew up in her family's convenience store, I would never want to make more work for a store's employees, but I knew what had to be done.

I picked her up, left the cart, and walked out of the store. By the time I put her in the car she was quieting down and still quite surprised that we had left the store. This meant I would have to go back another day and get everything, but I am convinced that clear, calm action helped put a quick end to her tantrums.

The second tantrum happened about a week later. We were at another family's home and there were lots of children. My daughter was used to playing with this family and always had a great time. I enjoyed the chance to talk with a wonderful, more experienced mom, so I had a great time too.

Just like in the store, my dear child turned into a loud, screaming, kicking, primal being. I looked at the other mother. She smiled. After taking a deep breath I said, "Goodbye." I picked up my wiggling, screaming child and walked out the door. Our home was a short walk away. As soon as we were in the house, I sat her on the bottom stair and said, "Come talk to me when you're ready." She stopped crying. As before, I think she was so surprised that I had just left the other house. No talking, no debate. She realized this was not acceptable behavior.

Does it work this well for every child and every circumstance? Of course not, but you will get the best results if you are consistent, calm, and have practiced a plan of action in your mind. One day I was tired and did not follow this advice. That's when my son had a tantrum.

We were both emotional and voices were raised. I wasn't following my own best advice. Instead of being calm and decisive, I was engaging in fruitless, repetitive arguments.

I stopped, took a deep breath and said, "I am going to my room for a time-out, and we will talk later when we are both calm."

He said, "I'm getting a time-out?"

"No," I said, "I am getting a time-out." I went to my room for a few minutes to calm down.

My son immediately calmed down. I think he couldn't believe it–Mom's in a time out? Well, parenting isn't perfect.

In our house, we used the term "time-out" a little differently. For us it is less of a punishment, and more of a, someone needs a few minutes alone to pull themselves together. And I needed a couple minutes to myself so I could be back to my old self. **Parenting is about knowing yourself as much as it is about knowing your child.**

Beyond Tantrums

I feel the need to reach out to those parents who find themselves with a real problem that many people don't understand or just blame on the parents. If your child is aggressive or violent, the sooner you deal with it the better - and you must be consistent.

Occasionally, a child will be extremely aggressive. There is not one reason for this type of behavior. The calmest, sweetest parents can have a strong aggressive, even violent child and wonder, *how did this happen?* A child can also be in a family with violent tendencies and then mimic those actions at home or at school. If you notice these tendencies in your child (this is beyond normal tantrums) it is imperative that you take action.

We are talking about a child who acts in anger. If a normal response to being told "No" is hitting, biting, yelling and an overall dismissal of the feelings and safety of others, you have a problem. I have known parents who were afraid of their preschooler. Imagine how scary it will be if those behaviors have not been addressed before the child is older and stronger.

Early professional help can change a family's life for the better. Your doctor or local social services can help you find the best help for your family. Helpful resources can be found at Loveandlogic.com

Further Reading for Parents

Potty Training:

Crane, Teri. *Potty Train Your Child in Just One Day: Proven Secrets of the Potty Pro*. (Touchstone Books, 2006).

Glowacki, Jamie. *Oh Crap! Potty Training: Everything Modern Parents Need to Know to Do It Once and Do It Right*. (Touchstone; First Paperback Edition, 2015).

Tantrums and Anger:

Goldstein, Sam PhD., Brooks, Robert PhD., Weiss, Sharon Med. *Angry Children, Worried Parents: Seven Steps to Help Families Manage Anger*. (Specialty Press/A.D.D. Warehouse, 2004

Greene, Ross W. PhD. *The Explosive Child: A New Approach for Understanding and Parenting Easily Frustrated, Chronically Inflexible Children*. (Harper Paperbacks, 2014).

Books to Share with Your Child

Potty Training:

Frankel, Alona. *Once Upon a Potty*. (Firefly Books; Brdbk edition, 2014).

Patricelli, Leslie. *Potty*. (Candlewick; Brdbk edition, 2010).

Tantrums and Anger:

Bang, Mollie. *When Sophie gets Angry--Really, Really Angry...* (Scholastic Paperbacks; Reprint edition 2004)

Spelman, Cornelia Maude. *When I Feel Angry*. (Whitman, Albert & Company, 2000).

Wonderful variations in preschool art.

9
THE ARTS AND EXPLORATION

Key Factors:

Music, painting, drawing, dancing, and tumbling help children grow and see things from different perspectives.

In order to create and assimilate information, children need uninterrupted time for exploration.

Drawing is a basic communication skill.

Painting is great for both large and small motor skills.

Three-dimensional art builds dexterity and problem-solving skills.

Play songs and music you love, not just children's songs.

Nursery rhymes and folk songs are a great way to introduce language and vocabulary.

It's best to keep a few nice rhythm instruments, like a drum, shakers, rhythm sticks, and a bell or triangle.

Dance and tumbling, whether it's gymnastics or wrestling on the floor, build more than just physical coordination.

Art requires time to come up with an idea, time to create something from that idea, and time to think about how you could have done it differently.

Minds, young and old, need time to process what they are learning.

∼

I would argue that the most valuable things to learn both for children and adults are those things that are often unquantifiable, like the arts. **Music, painting, drawing, dancing, and tumbling help children grow and see things from different perspectives.**

Any quality preschool will allow time for discovery through art, music, and movement. In this chapter, we will go over how these disciplines help your child and ways to incorporate some of them into your daily routines. Your child spends more time with you than he spends at school. Here are some ways to support and extend his learning, including what you can do that most schools cannot do to the same extent; extended, focused, alone time to explore and experiment.

Creative problem solvers are highly sought after as adults. Most children are naturally creative problems solvers. How do we help them keep and grow these skills that should be used throughout one's life? It is not uncommon for many children who enjoy the arts and physical games to stop pursuing these interests between the ages of 9 and 12. This is when self-criticism and the need to fit in can stop children from enjoying hobbies they once loved.

How do we prevent this from happening? One piece of the puzzle is to help them develop these skills as young children, so they do not feel awkward or insecure in these skills as they get older. Even some 4-year-olds will compare and criticize their own artwork. You can curb that behavior by asking your child questions about his artwork, rather than saying, "It's good," which really means nothing.

Try some of these: What is happening in your picture? Why did you choose red? How did you get all those shades of red? Look at all those colors. That looks like it's moving; is it? What happens if we turn it this way? Tell me about your painting.

In order to create and assimilate information, children need uninterrupted time for exploration. Remember in Chapter 5, when we were discussing developmental topics like motor skills, cognitive skills, language skills, and social skills? All of these skills can be developed through the arts. All of these skills require time for experimentation and discovery.

Drawing

Let's start with drawing. **Drawing is a basic communication skill.** In countries like Japan, drawing is considered a basic skill like writing, and it's a regular part of the school day. Like any other skill you get better at it the more you do it. Children and adults can get frustrated when they can't get what they see in their head onto the paper. It takes practice, but anyone can draw. Some basic guidance like Mona Brookes' book, *Drawing with Children: A Creative Method for Adult Beginners, Too,* can help.

For preschoolers, it takes time to experiment, and it's nice to try different drawing tools. Little hands that are just starting to work on fine motor skills do better with fat pencils and crayons. If your child seems frustrated with regular pencils or crayons, give those fat ones a try.

Drawing can be a very relaxing thing to do together. Maybe it was a sunny, fun day with lots of yellow swirls. Maybe it was a rainy grey day with lots of grey and black dots. If you are waiting somewhere with your child, be sure to bring along pencils or crayons and paper. Unlike toys that can get old, drawings are new each time.

If you are home or some place where you can be messy, nontoxic pastels, chalk, or charcoals are great to experiment with. I keep burnt wood from the fireplace (charcoal sticks) to use for drawing. Kids get very excited that you can draw with burnt sticks. It's a fun way to draw outside in warm weather.

Your child is not too young to draw from a still life. Don't worry about what that drawing looks like. The goal is to get the feel of the object. Put a flower or a seashell or a pinecone on the table and sit with your child to draw. It's about concentration and seeing. If he puts a couple spiky lines for the pinecone that's great. He is seeing the spikes. It will grow and change over time. Ask him to stare at the still life for 20 to 30 seconds before drawing anything on the paper. That takes practice for a child and maybe for you, too. Stare at the pinecone and you will see parts of it you hadn't noticed before.

Here are some things drawing does for your child. It develops control of fine motor skills. It engages your child's imagination. Over time, drawing helps your child to gain focus and concentration. Figuring out how to get what you want on the paper is a problem-solving skill that will develop through trial and error. Drawing with friends helps build camaraderie and helps children see things from another's perspective.

How about coloring? It's fun for everyone. Adult coloring books have become quite popular because coloring is relaxing. Children love to color with their parents. Remember to keep it fun. The few times my father colored with me when I was 4 or 5-years old, he was so concerned about coloring inside the lines and using the "right" colors, that it was no fun at all. Surely Princess Aurora should be green. I continued to color, but even as I grew older, it was rare for me to show my art to my father. Many children stop creating all together if they feel their pictures are being judged.

Painting and Three-Dimensional Art

Painting is both an extension of drawing and a creature of its own. The trick with painting is to have an easy set up and clean up so you will let your child regularly enjoy his creativity and you won't worry about the mess. A little planning makes all the difference. Maybe you have an area with a floor that is easy to clean, or a space outside.

I know a family that lets their children paint with nontoxic paints on the outside of their sliding glass door and then hoses it off. How fun is that? It also keeps the children focused on the fun of the process of painting rather than the product since they know the painting will be washed away.

Paints don't have to be messy. There is nothing wrong with a small cake (dried) watercolor set. Even a preschooler can pull out those paints, some water, and a brush to work on their own. Use a table that is easy to wipe off later or one that is just for art so it doesn't matter if paint gets on it.

Painting is great for both large and small motor skills. Set up a space with large paper and your child can really express himself. Painting will be a joy. Painting increases cognitive skills. Your child is learning physically and visually about colors, shapes, and sizes. You can add letter play to that list. Some children who are not ready to write with a pencil love to paint letters, their name, or other words.

Let's not forget three-dimensional art. Now your child is thinking. Talk about getting children to look at things in different ways. How do I bend the wire to look like a triangle or a dog? Is there a way to fold the strip of paper so it stands up, instead of lying flat on the page? **Three-dimensional art builds dexterity and problem-solving skills.**

Gluing found items and craft items onto a paper or cardboard gets children thinking about different ways to use materials. It's exciting to work with different textures and unusual materials, from acorns to wool. If you want to get those creative juices flowing, consider air-dry clay. It's clean, easy to use, and most children love to create shapes out of it. When it's dry, your child can paint it.

Pack a small bag with paper and art supplies so it's ready to go anytime you and your child have to sit and wait somewhere. At home a small box with supplies that he may use on his own will help with independence. It works best if he knows you consider the art box to be something special. Maybe he can help pick it out and decorate it himself. Some families reserve a box with special supplies for a weekly art session, but it's nice to keep supplies where your child can access them any time he has the creative urge.

Music

Hopefully music is already a part of your life. Some parents are so busy making time for their kids' music, they stop enjoying their own music. You should enjoy music too so, **play songs and music you love, not just children's songs.** Watch your mood perk up when you share music you enjoyed when you were younger, with your child. There are now so many ways to stream or access music that parents and children can enjoy together. If you don't subscribe to a streaming service, you can visit your local library.

Folk songs and nursery rhymes are often neglected with all of our modern gadgets and streaming devices. These songs not only give children a cultural background, but they are written so intervals (distances between pitches) and melodies are easy to sing. This makes them great for children who are learning to sing (and adults who think they can't sing well).

Nursery rhymes and folk songs are a great way to introduce language and vocabulary. You can find songs from around the world at https://allnurseryrhymes.com I bet you know many from when you were young, like *Mary had a Little Lamb* or *Hey Diddle Diddle.*

Now we just need to add instruments. You need nothing fancy, and you can find most of what you need in the kitchen. Wooden spoons and pots make great drums. Explore with your child to find other sounds. Keep a special music basket with some instruments appropriate for young children. Pull it down a couple afternoons a week to sing and play. Sometimes, not pulling that basket down every day makes it a special event. You can find good rhythm instruments for children online at *For Small Hands*. Here is the website... https://www.forsmallhands.com/music-1

Please do not buy cheap plastic instruments that insult your child's ears. **It's best to keep a few nice rhythm instruments, like a drum, shakers, rhythm sticks, and a bell or triangle.** You can add to your instrument collection as your child grows, which will keep the collection interesting and relevant.

There are some great classes for parents and children to share. My favorite music classes are *Music Together*, *Musikgarten*, and *Kindermusik*. They all have national websites and strong curricula. Meet the teacher before you start. Each program is only as good as the teacher, no matter what the advertisements say.

While we're singing, we're building language skills. We're working on physical coordination as we play instruments and when we move to the music. I would say this leads us to dancing. It's for everyone! You want to add dancing to your daily routine? How about whenever you're preparing a meal in the kitchen? That's one of my favorite times to play a fun song. Here's where you can get some of your music in and dance while you work. Don't let life's practical chores keep you from having fun. Lucky you, having a young child with you is a great excuse to dance in the grocery store or down the street.

Parents often ask, "At what age should I enroll my child in private music lessons?" There is no one answer to this question, but here are a few things to keep in mind. Between the ages of 5 and 7 years, group lessons are more fun and keep children interested in learning music. Check your area, many music teachers hold group keyboard classes that incorporate other instruments, singing, and movement.

Avoid pushing your child into individual lessons if they don't seem interested. You may keep them playing for a while, but they are likely to develop a hatred of music lessons. Likewise, if a teacher says she does not take children under a certain age (usually 7 or 10 years) honor that and do not ask for an exception for your child.

Music is taught very differently for children under 10. A frustrated teacher will turn your child away from music. It doesn't matter how wonderful a musician the teacher is if she does not know how to work with young children.

If your child loves music and wants to learn an instrument, try to follow your child's lead. Some early childhood music teachers will spend a year teaching general music and trying different instruments so the child and the teacher can find the best instrument fit. That said, piano or keyboard can be a great starter instrument as it gives a strong background in music theory while you are learning to play. You can see the musical scales, right there in front of you, not true on a recorder or a ukulele.

If your child wants to move on to another instrument after playing the piano, he did not waste time. The knowledge gained from the piano lessons will transfer to the new instrument. Students progress the most and continue the longest when they have a voice in instrument choice.

Movement

Dance is the physical extension of music. Learning to move to the beat builds coordination and strengthens a child's body. A strong internal sense of rhythm has been shown to enhance language skills. It's great exercise, and it's fun.

Dance and tumbling, whether it's gymnastics or wrestling on the floor, build more than just physical coordination. These activities build neural connections and strengthen muscles and organs. Children can pursue these interests in classes and later in performances and competitions. But even if your child is not interested in performing, learning to control your physical body in relation to space is an important skill.

When my children were young, we celebrated Swedish Midsummer every year. I mention this because two young adults who attended those parties, where everyone was asked to dance around the midsummer pole, told me how much they loved it and how they think of it every time they drive by our house. I hadn't seen them in years, but music and movement build memories. Be sure to add some to your family traditions. The years with your children go by too fast to worry about whether you are a wonderful dancer or singer. It's easy to improve your skills. Just join in!

Time to Explore

The title of this chapter is *The Arts and Exploration*. We covered a bit about the arts, but exploration is all about allowing your child and yourself time to think and take in what you have learned or seen. **Art requires time to come up with an idea, time to create something from that idea, and time to think about how you could have done it differently.** It requires time to figure out what you like about your work and what you can add to it.

It's important not to over schedule your child or yourself. Calm downtime is invaluable. **Minds, young and old, need time to process what they are learning.** Creativity flourishes after children pass the "I don't know what to do with myself," or the "I'm bored" stage. Letting a young child figure out how to pass the time or how to amuse themselves encourages creativity and helps create a peaceful inner life that is not dependent on constant distraction from others.

Many educators will tell you that children have the creativity educated out of them. Children are naturally creative problem solvers. To keep this going, we need to give children creative outlets and the time to explore them.

Further Reading for Parents

Brookes, Mona. *Drawing with Children: A Creative Method for Adult Beginners, Too.* (JP Tarcher, 1996).

Hannaford, Carla. *Smart Moves: Why Learning Is Not All in Your Head.* (Great River Books, 2007).

Louv, Richard. *Last Child in the Woods.* (Algonquin Books, 2008).

Nields, Katryna and Nields, Nerissa. *All Together Singing in the Kitchen: Creative Ways to Make and Listen to Music as a Family.* (Roost Books, 2011).

Snel, Eline. *Sitting Still Like a Frog: Mindfulness Exercises for Kids.* (Shambhala, 2013).

Books to Share with Your Child

Andreae, Giles. *Giraffes Can't Dance.* (Cartwheel Books; Broardbook edition, 2013).

Doherty, Kathleen. *The Thingity-Jig.* (Peachtree Publishing Company, 2021).

de la Peña, Matt; pictures by Robinson, Christian. *Milo Imagines the World.* (G.P. Putnam's Sons, 2021)

Portis, Antoinette. *Not A Box.* (HarperCollins Publishers, 2006).

Weiss, George David and Thiele, Bob. *What A Wonderful World.* (Atheneum Books for Young Readers, 1995). *This book is best when shown while playing a recording of the Louis Armstrong version of "What A Wonderful World."*

10

KINDERGARTEN

Key Factors:

Kindergarten is not just new for your child; it's new to all the kindergarten children.

We build friends and community by sharing new experiences.

Kindergarten teachers do their best to meet your child at her level, socially, cognitively, and physically, just like her preschool teacher did.

Many elementary schools have a playground where your soon-to-be-kindergartener can play during the summer so she can take ownership of her new school.

Many communities have a variety of choices for kindergarten.

Be careful not to make your life difficult before even trying your public school.

Don't underestimate the damage done to a local school system, when all the families that can afford private school leave. If your area has a good school system, your family will make the public school system stronger.

Enjoy all the growth and new abilities your child will gain as she moves into kindergarten.

Your child will be exhausted by the end of her new school day. Have snacks and patience waiting for her when she gets home.

Great! You've just about made it through preschool. Hopefully, all is well. You and your preschooler are happy, settled, loving the school routine, and suddenly, it's time to think about Kindergarten.

Although the transition to kindergarten comes with its own challenges, most children handle it very well with support from home. The transition from preschool to kindergarten can be worrisome for some parents. This is where you have to trust that your child is ready to go off on her own, often for a pretty long day.

Kindergarten is not just new for your child; it's new to all the kindergarten children. Many parents try to hold their young child back and phase in the change, often with unexpected consequences.

An example of this is riding the school bus. I have known many families who plan to have their child ride the school bus, but decide to drive their child to school for the first few days or weeks. What happens when their child finally rides the school bus? It can be a tough transition. All the other children have already been riding the bus. They are used to how it all works and they have found their place on the bus which often includes a friend to sit with.

It's better to let your child start on the bus, while it is still a new experience for all the other kindergarteners. **We build friends and community by sharing new experiences.**

Kindergarten is what you've been preparing for. Think of it as the next grand adventure. Remember that **kindergarten teachers do their best to meet your child at her level, socially, cognitively, and physically, just like her preschool teacher did.**

As long as you are an involved parent, things should go pretty smoothly, a little positive thinking and trust on your part can go a long way. Try to connect with the teacher early on so you will be a known entity if questions pop up. If the school has a kindergarten camp in the summer or even a day to meet the teacher, try to attend with your child.

Many families see the trend in pushing academics too early in school and wonder if they should hold their child back a year? Only you can answer this question. It has many variables, including the boredom your child may feel if she is too far ahead of her peers in school. The most important factor is your child's readiness. Maturity is much more important than chronological age.

Your child is your baby and may seem younger to you than she really is. You should ask your child's preschool teacher for his recommendation. If you still have concerns about your child's readiness, I would recommend contacting the elementary school. Ask if you can meet with one of the kindergarten teachers to get an honest assessment of kindergarten expectations at the school.

Kindergarten teachers are trained to make their subjects accessible to all kindergarteners and the children are all learning together. If you visit a kindergarten in the Spring, you need to remember those are not the expectations teachers had in the Fall! A few months make a big difference.

If your child is on track for kindergarten, try to go by the school so your child will feel familiar with the new school setting. **Many elementary schools have a playground where your soon-to-be-kindergartener can play during the summer so she can take ownership of her new school.** She may meet other kindergarteners on the playground. If you know of other children her age in the neighborhood, it can be helpful to have a couple play dates with those children so your child will see a familiar face at school.

Do not be surprised if your child is acting a little clingy as her preschool year gets closer to ending and she is thinking about kindergarten. Try not to make a huge deal about this transition at school, just answer her questions. Let her know she is ready to go to kindergarten.

Listen closely to your child's questions. One common misconception preschoolers have has to do with understanding the calendar. It is not unusual for a child to think kindergarten starts right after preschool ends. I spend a good amount of time at the end of the school year showing children visual representations of how long the summer break will be. Using a separate piece of paper for each week, I divide each paper into the seven days of the week. This allows me to show children how much time has to pass before Kindergarten starts. I try to clarify that it is some time away and they have all summer to enjoy first. For preschoolers who attend school through the summer this is less of a concern.

The transition into kindergarten is often much harder for parents than for children. It's easy to look for things your child might not like about school next year. I want to suggest that you don't look for problems. Remember, it's new for all the children and they will learn (and bond) together as they get used to their new school.

Many communities have a variety of choices for kindergarten beyond public school. But **be careful not to make your life difficult before even trying your public school.**

I have known several parents who listened to friends' concerns regarding the local public schools. Out of fear and worry, these families put their children into private schools without even considering the local public school. Several of those families ended up regretting their decision. If your child ends up in a private school you don't like, your child will have to transfer to another school. And it can be very expensive for you.

If you have a strong interest in education and your local schools, **don't underestimate the damage done to a local school system, when all the families that can afford private school leave. If your area has a good school system, your family will make the public school system stronger.**

If your school system is good, I suggest trying it first. Be part of your community. This is the same community your child will grow up in and perhaps work in one day. If the school is missing something you prize, like an art class, can you add that to your child's schedule outside of school? That would be easier than finding a new school. Be careful not to add afterschool activities until your child is used to her new Kindergarten schedule.

Children thrive on consistency. So, if you are planning to have your child attend the public school after kindergarten, then it will be easier for her to start and stay at the public school. You don't want every year to be a big transition.

All the previous comments are based on a solid public school system. Regardless of all the negative talk by politicians, there are many strong school systems in the United States. If you live in an area where public schools are just not safe, or if your child has special needs, you think will not be met, by all means, check into your options. It's always good to know what options are available. Just don't rule out a good option that is free before you've tried it. You'll be paying tuition soon enough.

There are talented educators and concerned parents working to change elementary education at the local level across the country. That's a whole different book. If you feel your local schools are on the wrong path, you may need to send your child to a private school. The most important thing you can do if this happens to you is to send a letter to your public school's principal and the local superintendent explaining why you have left the school system. Change only happens when enough people speak out. School administrators can't make changes without documentation.

To sum up, **enjoy all the growth and new abilities your child will gain as she moves into kindergarten.** If your child is voicing any fears, listen, but don't dwell on them. This is your child's next big step toward independence and making her own choices and friends.

All that learning takes a great deal of energy. **Your child will be exhausted by the end of her new school day. Have snacks and patience waiting for her when she gets home.** Your child might be crabby after school for the first couple months. Give her time to get used to the new schedule. It can be exhausting to meet all the new demands of school. A bit of attitude by the time she gets home is to be expected early in the year. It does not mean that anything is wrong at school.

Kindergarten is a special time of life. I hope you and your child have a wonderful time.

Books to Share with Your Child

Rogers, Jacqueline. *Tiptoe Into Kindergarten.* (Scholastic Cartwheel Books, 2003).

EPILOGUE

While writing *The Preschool Parent Primer*, I spent a little time visiting my cousin who lives on the Eastern Shore. As I sat on the pier one morning, I saw a feather floating in the water. It amazed me, the way the feather seemed to stay in the same place for so long, even though I knew it must be moving.

Parenting can be like that. It can seem like life is in a rut. Potty training is taking forever and you're exhausted. The feather seems to stay in one place. But when you look back, it was a brief moment in time. It seems like just when you've figured out a child's sleep pattern, it changes. A breeze comes along and moves the feather down the river.

Just know that parenting is about change and growth for child and parent. The best way to handle change is to get plenty of rest (both you and your child) so you can enjoy, change and grow together. Take in the moments. The feather will get to shore.

Enjoy time with your preschooler.

Preschool baking, Turtle Bread is done!

BIBLIOGRAPHY

Bronson, Po & Merryman, Ashley. *NurtureShock; New Thinking About Children.* (Hachette Book Group, 2009).

Brookes, Mona. *Drawing with Children: A Creative Method for Adult Beginners, Too.* (JP Tarcher, 1996).

Brown, Stuart & Vaughan, Christopher. *Play: How It Shapes the Brian, Opens the Imagination, and Invigorates the Soul.* (Penguin Group, 2009).

Carter, Christine. *Raising Happiness, 10 Simple Steps for More Joyful Kids and Happier Parents.* (Ballantine Books, 2011).

Christakis, Erika. *The Importance of Being Little: What Preschoolers Really Need From Grownups.* (Viking, 2016).

Crane, Teri. *Potty Train Your Child in Just One Day: Proven Secrets of the Potty Pro.* Touchstone Books, 2006).

Curtis, Deb and Carter, Margie, *Designs for Living and Learning: Transforming Early Childhood Environments.* (Redleaf Press, 2014).

Eanes, Rebecca. *Positive Parenting: An Essential Guide.* (Tarcher Perigee, 2016).

Edwards, Carolyn; Gandini, Lella; Forman, George; Editors. *The Hundred Languages of Children: The Reggio Emilia Approach – Advanced Reflections.* (Ablex Publishing Corporation, 1998).

Eisen, Andrew R., Engler, Linda B., Sparrow, Joshua. *Helping Your Child Overcome Separation Anxiety or School Refusal: A Step-By-Step Guide for Parents.* (New Harbinger Publications, Inc. 2006).

Fay, Jim. *Love and Logic Magic: When Kids Drain Your Energy.* (Love and Logic Institute, 2004).

Glowacki, Jamie. *Oh Crap! Potty Training: Everything Modern Parents Need to Know to Do It Once and Do It Right.* (Touchstone; First Paperback Edition, 2015).

Goldstein, Sam PhD., Brooks, Robert PhD., Weiss, Sharon Med. *Angry Children, Worried Parents: Seven Steps to Help Families Manage Anger.* (Specialty Press/A.D.D. Warehouse, 2004).

Greene, Ross W. PhD. *The Explosive Child: A New Approach for Understanding and Parenting Easily Frustrated, Chronically Inflexible Children.* (Harper Paperbacks, 2014).

Hannaford, Carla. *Smart Moves: Why Learning Is Not All in Your Head.* (Great River Books, 2007).

Healy, Jane M. *Your Child's Growing Mind: A Practical Guide to Brain Development and Learning from Birth to Adolescence.* (Broadway Books, 2004).

Louv, Richard. *Last Child in the Woods.* (Algonquin Books, 2008).

Lythcott-Haims, Julie. *How to Raise an Adult: Break Free of the Overparenting trap and Prepare Your Kid For Success.* (Henry Holt and Company, LLC, 2015).

Montessori, Maria. *The Montessori Method.* (Schocken Books, Inc., 1964).

Nields, Katryna and Nields, Nerissa. *All Together Singing in the Kitchen: Creative Ways to Make and Listen to Music as a Family.* (Roost Books, 2011).

Oppenheimer, Sharifa. *Heaven on Earth: A Handbook for Parents of Young Children.* (Steiner Books, 2006).

Pantley, Elizabeth. *The No-Cry Sleep Solution for Toddlers and Preschoolers.* (McGraw-Hill, 2005).

Petrash, Jack. *Understanding Waldorf Education: Teaching from the Inside Out.* (Gryphon House, 2002).

Siegel, Daniel J. and Bryson, Tina Payne. *The Whole Brain Child: 12 Revolutionary Strategies to Nurture Your Child's Developing Mind.* (Delacorte Press, Random House Publishing Group, 2011).

Snel, Eline. *Sitting Still Like a Frog: Mindfulness Exercises for Kids (and Their Parents).* (Shambhala, 2013).

Ward, Jennifer. *I Love Dirt.* (Trumpeter Books, an imprint of Shambhala Publications, Inc., 2008).

Young, Jon; McGown, Evan; Haas, Ellen. Coyote's Guide to Connecting with Nature. (Owlink Media, 2010).

RECOMMENDED CHILDREN'S STORIES

Andreae, Giles. *Giraffes Can't Dance*. (Cartwheel Books; Brdbk edition, 2013).

Appelt, Kathi. *Oh My Baby, Little One*. (Harcourt Children's Books, 2006).

Bang, Mollie. *When Sophie gets Angry--Really, Really Angry...* (Scholastic Paperbacks; Reprint edition 2004).

Beskow, Elsa. *Peter's Old House*. (Floris Books, 1990).

Boston, Marc. *The Girl Who Carried Too Much Stuff*. (Juju Seeds Media, LLC. 2015).

Cohen, Miriam and Himler, Ronald. *Will I Have a Friend* (Star Bright Books, 2009).

Cornwall, Gaia, *Jabari Jumps*, (Candlewick, 2017).

Doherty, Kathleen. *The Thingity-Jig*. (Peachtree Publishing Company, 2021).

Frankel, Alona. *Once Upon a Potty*. (Firefly Books; Brdbk edition, 2014).

Meddaugh, Susan. *Cinderella's Rat*. (Houghton Mifflin Company, 1997).

Northway, Jennifer. *See you later Mum*! (Frances Lincoln Children's Books, 2006).

Patricelli, Leslie. *Potty*. (Candlewick; Brdbk edition, 2010).

de la Peña, Matt; pictures by Robinson, Christian. *Milo Imagines the World*. (G.P. Putnam's Sons, 2021)

Penn, Audrey. *The Kissing Hand*. (Tanglewood Press, Inc., 2006).

Portis, Antoinette. *Not A Box*. (HarperCollins Publishers, 2006).

Pova, Rosie J. *Sunday Rain*. (Lantana Publishing Ltd. 2021)

Robinson, Christian. *You Matter*. (Atheneum Books for Young Readers, 2020).

Spelman, Cornelia Maude. *When I Feel Angry*. (Whitman, Albert & Company, 2000).

Weiss, George David and Thiele, Bob. *What A Wonderful World*. (Anthenum Books for Young Readers, 1995). *This book is best when shown while playing a recording of the Louis Armstrong version of "What A Wonderful World."*

ACKNOWLEDGMENTS

Many thanks to all my editors, advance readers, and book contributors, your input was invaluable; Carolyn O'Neal, JoAnn Evans, Julie Baird, Dianne Bearinger, Darailia Evans, Heather Swindler, and Camille Wilson.

The Preschool Parent Primer is the culmination of decades of teaching so I must thank my many students and a special thank you to the inspirational families of *C-Street Cooperative Preschool.*

Thanks to Ben for keeping me on track and to my favorite I.T. guy G.W. "Did you try turning it off and turning it back on again?"

I would like to express my gratitude to the following programs, administrators, and teachers for their advice and photographs for this edition of *The Preschool Parent Primer*...

>   *Nicole Brin, Assistant Director*
>   *Schuylkill Center for Environmental Education*
>   *8480 Hagy's Mill Road*
>   *Philadelphia, PA 19128*

http://www.schuylkillcenter.org

Jennifer Slack, Director
Our Neighborhood Child Development Center
1015 East Market Street
Charlottesville, VA, VA 22902
http://ourneighborhoodcdc.com

Karen Madigan, Director
The Nature Preschool, Irvine Nature Center
11201 Garrison Forest Road
Owings Mills, MD 21117
https://www.explorenature.org

Carolyn Schuyler, Founder
Wildrock, Nature Playscape
6700 Blackwells Hollow Road
Crozet, VA 22932
https://www.wildrock.org

Marty Watson, Preschool Director
Dodge Nature Preschool
1715 Charlton Street
West Saint Paul, MN 55118
http://www.dodgenaturecenter.org

ABOUT THE AUTHOR

Pamela Evans is a teacher, author, and artist. She lives by the Blue Ridge Mountains of Virginia. Her background in the arts and education includes work at Carnegie Hall, Disney World, The American Symphony Orchestra League, and Equity Library Theatre-NYC. As a teacher and school director, she has developed and run many programs for children including classes for the Saturday Enrichment Program at UVA Curry School of Education and curricula for special needs students. Pamela is a member of the National Association for the Education of Young Children (NAEYC) and the North American Association for Environmental Education (NAAEE).

Contact Pamela at info@IvyArtz.com
www.IvyArtz.com

 facebook.com/Author.Artist.Teacher.PamelaEvans
 twitter.com/PamelaEvans_Bks
 instagram.com/Pamela_Evans_Author

www.ingramcontent.com/pod-product-compliance
Lightning Source LLC
Chambersburg PA
CBHW071714090426
42738CB00009B/1769